Gaslighting

A Step-by-step Recovery Guide to Heal from Emotional Abuse Gas lighting

(Revealing Look at Psychological Manipulation and Narcissistic Abuse)

Jason Morgan

I0136066

Published By **Elena Holly**

Jason Morgan

Gaslighting: A Step-by-step Recovery Guide to Heal from Emotional Abuse Gas lighting (Revealing Look at Psychological Manipulation and Narcissistic Abuse)

ISBN   978-1-7774976-0-6

Legal & Disclaimer

The information contained in this book is not designed to replace or take the place of any form of medicine or professional medical advice. The information in this book has been provided for educational & entertainment purposes only.

The information contained in this book has been compiled from sources deemed reliable, and it is accurate to the best of the Author's knowledge; however, the Author cannot guarantee its accuracy and validity and cannot be held liable for any errors or omissions. Changes are periodically made to this book. You must consult your doctor or get professional medical advice before using any of the suggested remedies, techniques, or information in this book.

Table Of Contents

Chapter 1: Emotional Abuse And Why It Is Difficult To Recognize

Perhaps the largest mission with emotional abuse is which you not often expect it is able to be happening to you. We can examine about it and watch films or TV indicates approximately characters experiencing it. We sympathize with them and curse their abusers, but it in no way takes place to us that we can be experiencing the same trouble, albeit in a considered one of a type context. In fact, a close to friend might be telling you that they're experiencing emotional abuse in a dating with a determine or lover, describing quite a whole lot the same topics that appear to you day by day, and you continue to can also fail to understand that you're inside the equal boat. Does that imply that you're now not clever sufficient or that you're silly? Not at all. It actually technique that your thoughts is attempting to protect you.

Moreover, emotional abuse could be very difficult to apprehend. It's subtle and seldom felt clearly, and the manipulators who lodge to this shape of abuse apprehend it. They comprehend that it's not clean if you need to affirm which you're laid low with intellectual or emotional abuse. You can also moreover get a experience within the pit of your belly that some element is incorrect. You also can moreover enjoy that you're not happy or that the character abusing you isn't treating you proper. But emotional abuse eats at your conceitedness and changes the way you understand yourself. Instead of confronting your abuser at the side of your doubts and pain, you begin to doubt yourself and

2

suppose that the hassle may additionally lie with you. It doesn't.

Everyone is prone to experiencing emotional abuse. It doesn't decide who you are as someone, and it doesn't make you prone. You can be a completely sturdy-willed individual and though fall for a person who may also use your love for them to abuse you emotionally. They will make you think that you're the trouble and want to trade because it's you who's poisoning the connection whilst you're the victim in reality. After identifying a sample of toxic behavior that makes you uncomfortable, leaving can also although be too tough and often proves to be the toughest step for numerous humans. Here's why.

Why Leaving Emotionally Abusive People Is Hard

Gaslighting

We'll get to gaslighting in a piece, but for now, you want to understand that gaslighting makes walking away an awful lot extra difficult. The manipulator will accuse you of overreacting and growing tension in the relationship. They will plant the seeds of doubt to your mind and reason you to impeach your very very own sanity. Over time, even though you hate it, and it makes you uncomfortable, you may start to normalize dangerous and poisonous behavior, so you wouldn't be referred to as "unreasonable" or "annoying."

Feeling Trapped

One detail manipulators do very well is make you experience trapped, like there's no longer some aspect and no individual higher searching forward to you to be had. They continuously paintings on destroying your self-esteem to get you to some extent in which their abuse can also experience everyday for you, and you may downplay their abuse or perhaps occasionally don't forget it as endearment or their manner of expressing affection. "They're simply kidding.

It's their manner of goofing spherical," you could say at the same time as your accomplice insults you. This non-prevent sample makes you revel in that that's what a normal relationship seems like and that you can't do better while in truth, you cannot remarkable do better, but you deserve higher.

No Physical Violence

Another powerful purpose why leaving emotional abusers is tough and complex is the fact that they may in no manner bodily harm you. Emotional abuse can be accompanied via physical violence, however that is not constantly the case, and those are the extra diffused varieties of abuse that confuse a number of humans. In many times, human beings don't understand that they're being abused due to the fact no physical violence is being committed toward them. Even individuals who begin critically thinking about the opportunity that they may be experiencing emotional abuse often downplay it and declare that it's now not as

5

awful as bodily abuse. Years of non-prevent assaults to your arrogance can in the long run make you feel nugatory and can make you genuinely do not forget that there isn't anything better available. You begin to be thankful that your associate isn't hitting you each day, and also you convince yourself that emotional abuse isn't half of of of as awful as physical abuse, which makes leaving all the extra complicated.

Love Bombing

Serial abusers are very smart with their preliminary approach. "Love bombing" is when they shower you with love, affection, or maybe gadgets on the begin of a courting to earn your agree with and construct a connection. This makes it a fantastic deal more difficult in the future so that it will technique their emotional abuse for the purpose that your mind is going lower returned to that preliminary satisfactory treatment and the way they showered you with affection. You might also additionally have fallen so deeply in love that their toxic behavior will be tolerated and regular as a part of the package deal. Some people even do it by accident. They don't want to be serial abusers. At the start of any dating, it's normal to be to your first rate behavior and to act with love and affection to advantage the individual's don't forget. The actual trouble takes location when the alternative issue of their individual indicates, and it turns out to be a poisonous one. When encountered with this – regularly unexpected – exchange in conduct, patients try to be on the abuser's correct issue once more. They count on that they did something incorrect, and it became the purpose why the loving, affectionate individual they have been given to satisfy and love a while within the past has changed. In reality, the abuser is in reality displaying their proper color after captivating you into falling for them.

What makes matters worse is the fact that abusers will pass again to showering you with love after a big fight in which they abused and insulted you. They apprehend it's the manner to keep you hooked, in order that they do something notable and express regret, possibly even buy you some element to make up for his or her preceding conduct. They will promise you that they'll in no way do it over again, so you should forgive them and go along with the drift on and take into account their state-of-the-art abuse as a one-time incident. Unfortunately, it hardly ever proves to be a one-time incident. Before you're privy to it, you're in a vicious cycle that repeats itself often. They abuse you, topics make bigger, you enjoy unhappy or irritated, and then they bathe you with need to win you decrease lower back. Before prolonged, they abuse you all all over again, and the cycle begins offevolved offevolved throughout. This is why a whole lot of human beings turn out to be conflicted approximately leaving.

The Long-Term Nature of Emotional Abuse

At the begin of a courting, we have a tendency to disregard pink flags - symptoms and signs and symptoms that the person we're worried with might not be a exceptional character and perhaps an abuser. This complicates things down the street and makes it lots harder to stroll away later. On the alternative hand, abuse doesn't constantly seem overnight. Emotional abusers usually have a tendency to abuse their sufferers over years in location of in the quick term. It can also additionally start as playful jokes insulting your cooking abilties or your weight, and you could even snort on the side of them before the whole lot. Over the years, even in case you higher your self and change into the better version that your associate claimed they wanted, the jokes obtained't forestall. An abuser will discover some difficulty else to mock. The jokes emerge as derogatory remarks geared closer to destroying your vanity and declaring your already modern-day insecurities to make you extra obedient. If you object and attempt to ask your accomplice to be extra supportive in place of mocking and cruel, they'll allow you to realise which you stopped being amusing and also you're taking matters manner too significantly. "Lighten up, it's a comic story," they'll say, however after years of experiencing the same insults and threatening remarks underneath the guise of jokes, that this isn't finished in humor. It's an try and control you and weaken your solve, thereby decreasing your arrogance.

Distance from Friend and Family

In the presence of a assist machine, emotional abuse will become lots much less effective, and your abuser has lots an awful lot much less sway over you. Having pals and circle of relatives folks that love you manual you makes a wonderful distinction. They communicate to you and pay interest, and that they assist you understand which you're no longer a horrific person and deserve higher. With their help, your insecurities are historical past noise, and that they don't manage your moves and reactions as plenty. This is why quite some abusers are in search of to distance you from family and friends.

They recognize that the ones loved ones will let you see subjects from a super mindset and understand that your relationship is unstable.

The abuser will let you know that it's simply the two of you closer to the area, and the two of you don't want everyone else. They will make up issues and let you know they don't like a specific pal of yours, an insightful person who in all likelihood warned you against the abuser early on on your dating. They will claim that your circle of relatives doesn't like them and is inflicting a rift on your courting. Over the years, your connection to your own family will reduce, and their presence on your lifestyles will fade, consequently making the abuser's manipulate over you tons greater effective. Without a assist circle, breaking far from an abusive courting is lots more tough, but you could however do it, and you can normally discover guide systems in case you try.

Social Pressure

Another number one element that contributes to patients staying in abusive relationships for a long time is the strain put forth via society to be in the ideal courting. You start wondering that you want to make the relationships paintings and work through the problems. Emotional abuse isn't the kind of trouble a couple can art work via. It's a sample of manipulation and an attack in your highbrow health that must no longer be tolerated beneath any instances, least of all to appease a cruel society that does not in fact deal with your properly-being. This shape of strain is amplified by way of conservative societies setting too much charge on notions of marriage and 'sticking together for higher or for worse.'

A lot of organizations try and perpetuate a subculture of sticking along with your accomplice or abusive discern no matter what because of a few faulty feel of entitlement that tries to steer you which you owe your abusers a few aspect. This kind of toxic notion is in addition perpetuated with the resource of people who undergo all of it to 'journey or die' for their pals as despite the fact that being a superb buddy method accepting abuse and ordinary mockery from considered absolutely certainly one of your so-referred to as friends. This absurd emphasis on notions of loyalty guilt-trips quite some human beings into staying in abusive relationships and friendships lest they be dubbed disloyal. You need to take into account that a terrific buddy or accomplice might in no way positioned you in a function in which you want to select out amongst your highbrow health and theirs. They should never manage or emotionally abuse you, now not to mention gaslight you while you confront them approximately how they harm you.

Genuine Affection for Abusers

As said earlier, in masses of times, we do have actual affection for our abusers. Maybe we hold in thoughts how they had been on the start of the connection earlier than they changed into an ugly model of themselves.

Perhaps we see the fine in them in desire to all the terrible. There are a million reasons for it, but the unhappy fact stays. In commonly, you like your abusive associate or a discern or pal who has in no way been some thing but mean and cruel in the direction of you subsequently of the time you've diagnosed them. This is probably the maximum complicated of feelings absolutely everyone should face, and it makes walking away from all of the more tough. You can have to triumph over your affection on your abuser and spot them for what they certainly are and how they make you revel in in order that you will be unfastened from their manipulate.

The hassle with having a deep connection to someone who happens to be an abuser is that it makes you fall into the trap of rationalization. Whenever they hurt you and control you, you find out yourself rationalizing the incident and trying to come up with a purpose for why subjects executed out the way they did. The fact that emotional abusers aren't frequently abusive 24/7 makes it more tempting to try and rationalize it while they may be, even extra so once they express regret and bathe you with love, as we described whilst discussing 'love bombing.'

Sharing a Life

Many humans come to the unlucky attention that they may be in abusive relationships, and that they realize that they want to go away, but it's not smooth if you percent a life along with your abuser. Having children collectively makes it even greater difficult to try to stroll away. Many women live with abusive husbands because of the reality they worry what their separation might also do to their kids, particularly if the father's abuse includes moderate, which could psychologically scar youngsters at a more youthful age. Moreover, sharing finances additionally complicates topics. It's extra than likely that the emotional abuser sought to keep the joint assets of their name and took control of every occasions' price range. Many humans dread the eventual separation and the prolonged court tactics really in order to get what's rightfully theirs, so that they stay round. This form of dependency may be very debilitating, and abusers understand it.

Fear for Safety

The sad reality is sometimes, it's certainly too risky to go away. Even in case to procure here to understand the terrible reality of your relationship and summoned the braveness to head away, it may be dangerous to stroll faraway from an abuser. Many human beings fear for his or her lives after they maintain in thoughts the selection to head away an abusive relationship, as it is able to be lifestyles-threatening in a few times. Breaking up with an abuser brings out an incredible worse component of them that might on occasion be violent and cruel. People who have had emotional and/or physical control over someone for a long time don't need to allow pass and emerge as desperate to manipulate the connection. Women are the most likely victim within the ones cases, and that they're 70 times more likely to be killed after leaving an abusive companion. The statistics right here are scary and show that guys have a propensity to be violent even as they are the abusers and regularly lash out on the same time as their partners depart.

These are the reasons why on foot some distance from abusers isn't easy and why it can be extraordinarily hard to understand types of emotional abuse. Reading this, you is probably gambling dozens of incidents on your head concerning one specific man or woman or severa for your lifestyles. To assist you get there, to find out in case you're in reality in an abusive relationship, we are able to define the kinds of poisonous behavior you will in all likelihood come across and dismiss as everyday. Remember that one of the abuser's most powerful weapons is normalization. Just due to the reality a high pleasant conduct has constantly been there for your courting doesn't suggest it's regular or brand new. So, while you begin identifying some of those poisonous patterns, take be conscious, and pay attention whilst next it takes place.

Types of Toxic Behavior and Emotional Abuse

Mockery and Put-Downs

No one is announcing banter isn't allowed amongst pals, family, and companions. Your husband teasing you that the meals has too much salt and which you're cooking talents need honing might be super if done in the consolation of your house after supper, as soon as in a blue moon. Your husband did that when you have friends or circle of relatives over is a unique story. If they're searching for to embarrass you in the front of your family and in the event that they're placing you down in public casually, some detail is wrong. Public humiliation is one of the most commonplace varieties of emotional abuse, and it want to in no manner be widespread. Your companion should love and recognize you normally, and disrespecting you inside the front of others is not a sign of affection or understand.

Constant mockery is some issue else to keep in mind. A decide continuously making fun of your hair, weight, profession options, love pastimes, and pretty much everything to your existence is emotionally abusing you. Again, don't confuse this with banter or a discern's authentic difficulty. A certainly concerned decide wouldn't call you a failure or mock your love lifestyles just for the fun of it. No one should make consistent jokes at your price, especially in public and in the the front of human beings you apprehend and care about. This need to undermine each person's vanity and make you experience which incorporates you're worthless. Being subjected to years of mockery and placed-downs is sufficient for absolutely everyone to absolutely start believing the phrases being stated. You may be a worldwide-elegance chef and start to keep in mind that you can't cook and you're a failure in case your accomplice continuously mocks your cooking and claims that your achievement changed right into a fluke.

Verbal Abuse and Intimidation

Emotional abuse is a sequence of types in which one kind outcomes within the alternative. Mockery and public humiliation almost continually bring about verbal abuse and intimidation. When your partner has no troubles calling you incompetent in front of your own family or mocking your weight/form/appearance, they'll possibly development to flat-out calling you silly and an imbecile in a few unspecified time in the future to your courting. Insults and verbal abuse should in no way be tolerated or normalized among couples, buddies, coworkers, or circle of relatives. Your boss constantly calling you stupid, a failure, incompetent, and other names are the very definition of verbal abuse. No one wants to lose their hobby, yes, however you need to understand that via manner of enduring this type of behavior, you're making it possible for them to do more than call-calling, and also you furthermore allow others to do the equal. If your boss can verbally abuse you and stroll away with it, why can't others? You start letting specific humans verbally abuse you, and your vanity plummets.

Constant swearing at you is verbal abuse, and it is intimidation, too. A partner who swears and loses their mood at you could do worse, and they'll and probably will go with the flow directly to hit you. They will often say hurtful phrases to interrupt you and bully you so that you wouldn't object to some element they're pronouncing. Using the husband/boyfriend instance again considering that this is the most popular if they call you stupid and you object, they will convey up situations in which you in all likelihood did some issue wrong. They will say and do something to undermine your self-self belief so you wouldn't be able to object to their insult. They also can even make subjects up, and also you won't have the capacity to inform due to the truth you're on an emotional rollercoaster. This will lead to a cycle of abuse, call-calling and insults, and steady attempts to undermine you.

Emotional abusers are, in maximum times, bullies. They will cope with you as if you're not so exact as them, and they'll do the whole thing in their electricity to strive to show it to you. They will blame you for everything, which include their private mistakes and shortcomings. If you object, they'll snap at you and intimidate you. They will continuously mock your ideas and opinions and tell you they're no longer well well worth tons. Whenever they've got a chance, they may let you recognise which you're wrong and could go out in their way to reveal it. Their tone with you can constantly be sarcastic and mocking because of the truth they consider you as inferior, and that they'll talk and act consequently. They will act like they understand great and as even though they're a splendid deal smarter than you. These are the styles of things an emotional abuser will say and do, all speculated to vicinity you down and intimidate you.

Blackmail

One of the maximum dangerous styles of emotional abuse that you need to take note of is blackmail, specifically, emotional blackmail. Not all emotional abusers are sincere or lodge to insults and intimidation as their crucial tactic. There are manipulative types in case you need to try to make you experience chargeable for expressing frustration or pain because of how they treated you. They apprehend the way to stability being hurtful and disrespectful to you with simply sufficient emotion to play the sufferer and act damage whilst you confront them. They emotionally blackmail you and turn the tables with the aid of claiming which you don't love, recognize, and/or cost them.

What makes topics worse is how they use your personal fears and values in opposition to you. They recognize you, and that they apprehend your triggers and are well aware about which nerves to strike to take manage of the scenario in an effort to turn it to their advantage. They want to take advantage of human beings's compassion and empathy, that is why women are extra frequently patients of emotional abuse than guys. They use them to make you experience responsible till you forget about about what dissatisfied you within the first vicinity and begin to express regret as even though it had been your fault inside the first place. One of the worst subjects they do is withhold affection as a form of blackmail until you begin to mellow and attempting to find out their love and affection. They'll essentially provide you with the silent treatment until you start feeling lonely and unloved.

Another form of blackmail is monetary, which moreover happens to women extra than men. The abuser can withhold money till you do their bidding, and they will go as an prolonged way as to save you you from going for walks or studying. This type of abuse is considered domestic violence, and it's just any other way for them to govern you and assert their dominance in the relationship.

Isolation Remember what we stated in advance about the abuser looking to limit the impact of your useful aid circle on you? They regularly try to isolate you from buddies and own family so that you must revel in all by myself and remoted. The trouble is that people often reply within the same way at the same time as handled poorly with the aid of someone they care approximately, this means that your friends and own family can develop remote when they sense which you're cold to them. Your abuser needs that to occur so that you begin to feel that they're the nice person you've got were given left, similarly preserving their manipulate over your existence.

Pay hobby to how your companion, determine, pal, or coworker treats and speaks approximately your family. Do they generally seem to have a problem with someone? Do they explicit distaste for first-rate vital people on your life? Do they take some time to get to recognize them, or are they dismissive of even the perception? These are all factors that you need to be aware of as they will show off whether or not or now not or not this person is making an attempt to strain-isolate you out of your social circles. Sometimes, things aren't so subtle, and the abuser is apparent with their choice to isolate you. They will show your personal chats, emails, and get in touch with log and control who you communicate with. They will claim you can't speak with positive people due to the reality they're a terrible have an effect on. They will tell you they're jealous, and all they want is to guard you. They will invade your privacy whenever feasible below the pretense of affection. They will take away the car keys and take your coins so you wouldn't be capable of pass go to others who might in all likelihood burst the bubble of fear and manage they stress you to live in.

If you try to object, they'll accuse you of cheating and being disloyal. They will commonly name for to understand in which you're at as though they're a jail warden and you're an inmate. They will try to pressure you to spend all of your time with them and claim that it's due to the reality they love you. As more time passes, you'll examine that your social life is lack of life, and you not have contact with pals or family. Your complete existence revolves round your abuser, who constantly claims that their best trouble is your well being. They will coerce you into staying far from absolutely everyone else who would in all likelihood take care of you really so they will be capable of stay on top of things of the relationship and contact the pics.

To top all of it, abusers will gaslight you all of the time. We will dive in-depth into gaslighting in the upcoming monetary wreck, however it virtually method that they will have you ever ever question your fact and your emotions and thoughts. Abusers will motive you to live in worry, and also you'll usually feel threatened. Abusers are professional manipulators and may drift as an prolonged manner as threatening to harm themselves when they're dissatisfied with you so you'll backpedal. Even if you're not scared of them harming you, you may be frightened of them doing some component to themselves. At the cease of the day, it's the identical final consequences. You're residing in worry, and also you constantly experience threatened. You sense that a few issue will always skip wrong if you express your self and speak approximately how their movements have an impact on you. As a cease end result, you bottle it up and swallow your pain and frustration.

These behaviors and patterns are matters which you need to be aware of. These aren't one-time gives. If a person bullies or intimidates and isolates you as fast as, they'll do it again. We will dive into how you could harm free from people who are this toxic later in the e-book, but for now, you virtually want to recognize these styles. The first step of solving a trouble is acknowledging that it exists. If you're in a relationship wherein this kind of behavior is regular, you want to prevent and endure in thoughts that you might be stricken by emotional abuse.

Chapter 2: Gaslighting

Gaslighting is a shape of emotional abuse, and it's arguably the maximum unstable kind as it makes you 2nd-wager your non-public mind. Gaslighting is a sort of intellectual manipulation wherein the abuser makes you query your judgment, reminiscence, and/or perception of things. Psychologists often warn approximately this form of manipulation and bear in thoughts it to be a completely immoderate element. The trouble with gaslighting is the reality that it is regularly very subtle and deceptive. Victims of gaslighting ought to likely in the long run experience that they may be, in reality, losing their sanity and belief of truth.

Another form of abusive manipulate, gaslighting, takes vicinity most customarily amongst couples, but it isn't one-of-a-type to relationships and may seem between friends, own family people, and coworkers. The danger of gaslighting is that it can bring about you losing your grip on truth and thinking your private mind, neither of which ever ends nicely. If someone close to you continuously questions and denies your version of sports, you can begin to be given as real with them and discredit your tale over the years.

How Gaslighting Works

Gaslighting regularly begins offevolved offevolved small with minor incidents that you can not located an lousy lot belief into, however they do deliver large outcomes ultimately. The activities where you have got been made to impeach your mind and your perception of factors in the slightest are dangerous, and they pile up ultimately. It may be some thing as simple as arguing alongside aspect your accomplice about who out of region the TV guide. You recognize for a reality that they have got been the remaining ones analyzing it, but while faced with it, your partner denies it. They say that it grow to be you who was closing reading the manual. They point out unique data like you putting ahead a particular application which you preferred to examine, or they're announcing which you have been reading it to your preferred chair on the time in which you typically have a cup of espresso with some component to look at. This diploma of specificity can confuse every person and will have you ever questioning if it'd were you who observe the manual and forgot approximately it. Your partner will remind you of yet again in which you have been forgetful to expose their thing, and it'll further instill in you the perception that this became your fault and you simply forgot.

This minor incident might seem inconsequential, however you want to apprehend that this is an incident wherein you basically didn't agree with your very very very own eyes. Your partner made you persuade your thoughts that it was your fault, and that they did it intentionally clearly to keep away from duty and escape the responsibility. An come upon with a gaslighter typically ends with you feeling rather tired and exhausted. You're dazed and compelled, unsure of what truly took place. It's nearly as in case you had a blackout and did some issue at the same time as you were genuinely unaware. You begin to wonder if there's a few component wrong with you, and you can probably don't forget getting your self checked out, all due to the reality your associate didn't want to take responsibility and alternatively gaslighted you into believing that it changed into your fault.

This shape of toxic conduct may want to have an effect for your highbrow well-being shifting ahead. As you pass about your everyday responsibilities and responsibilities, you're now not inside the right headspace. You doubt your self and 2d-bet your picks. If you forgot about some detail and accused your companion of doing it once they, in fact, did it, but they proved that it was your fault, what's preventing you from doing all of it another time? Your selection-making ability turns into impaired, and you're a far plenty much less confident version of yourself after years of being subjected to gaslighting.

Gaslighting Techniques Used by using Abusers

Discrediting You

Many abusers use this gaslighting method to advantage further manage inside the courting. They don't without a doubt discredit you for your face, however in addition they do it inside the back of your once more, spreading rumors and lies to others. They will explicit disingenuous venture to others— possibly mutual buddies and/or circle of relatives–and inform them that they think you're not properly. You've been tormented by bouts of intellectual instability, and it's impairing your judgment. They will claim which you're emotionally volatile and may even circulate as some distance as calling you 'loopy' or 'losing your thoughts.' This is not finished absolutely to hassle you however instead as a preemptive try and discredit you inside the the front of your family. This way, whilst you communicate to the ones human beings approximately how your companion is gaslighting you, they received't consider you, and they will function your version of the truth to what they've already been advised approximately your intellectual state.

In the long time, and after months or years of your abuser spreading gossip and fake information about you in the back of your all over again, you in the long run find out that humans you care approximately and look to for guide are siding with the very person who's gaslighting and abusing you. They don't understand the entire story, and that they've simply been getting fake records approximately your mental usa, it's miles why they don't consider you at the same time as you in the end visit them for help. This approach may be very powerful, and pretty some abusers use it. They moreover attempt to widen the rift among you and those people via way of telling you that those people already assume this manner approximately you. The abuser will tell you that your pals and own family recognize which you are mentally risky, and you've been making insane claims for a long term.

As extra time is going with the useful resource of way of, you experience an increasing number of remoted. If your accomplice believes it, and now your buddies and circle of relatives, perhaps what the abuser is saying approximately you is the reality. Maybe you're mentally or emotionally volatile, and also you've been the simplest liable for the connection going sour. See wherein this is going? This type of manipulative conduct is dangerous and might lead patients to lose their minds and absolutely remember that they may be insane.

The Lies

A gaslighter who does it constantly is thru nature a pathological liar. They don't expect instances about mendacity to you or making up exchange versions of the reality as prolonged as it serves their purpose and lets in them further convince you that the trouble is for your head. They haven't any qualms lying to your face, and that they constantly double down at the lies as even though it were the handiest and handiest truth. They realise that it isn't the fact, and that they apprehend that they're mendacity, however this self belief is complex and will have you query your self, which furthermore they recognize. It doesn't remember if you name them out on their lies or even provide evidence in their deceit. They will although declare that it's on your head and which you trust this.

Pathological lying is going hand in hand with gaslighting. The abuser will let you know that "you're making this up" and that what you're pronouncing "by no means passed off." It's every infuriating and mindboggling how someone can flat out deny some thing that you're 100% sure occurred. However, gaslighters do it, and they in no way go into reverse. As a surrender result of this unwavering self guarantee, you begin to see their model of the reality as what absolutely occurred, and you question your issue of things because of the truth in the event that they're this confident, why can't the issue that's horrifying you be all on your head? Lying is a pillar of this toxic behavior, and with out it, the gaslighter has no power over you. You nonetheless need to keep in mind, despite the fact that, that their lies have strength over you only if you offer it to them.

Using the Power Dynamic

In most instances, gaslighting is intently associated with the energy dynamic of a relationship. The abuser holds the higher hand for one purpose or the other, as an example, male strength given through society, and they use that to leverage the power dynamic into maintaining you underneath their manage. You become accustomed to this imbalanced energy dynamic, and also you're fearful of breaking freed from it as that freedom is associated with the hazard of losing the relationship. This is why your thoughts wants to bear in mind the lies and half of of-truths the abuser is telling you. It desires to maintain the relationship and maintain the electricity dynamic in a possibly uncomfortable but pretty familiar reputation quo. Abusers recognize this all too nicely and feed you the lies that they understand will maintain you continuously thinking things until you finally decide to paste around.

Distractions

Manipulative as they will be, abusers and gaslighters are not infallible. They will now not definitely use gaslight and mislead you, but they may additionally try to distract you and maintain you in a regular kingdom of chaos so you by no means get within the path of the reality. When you confront them about their abuse or regarding an incident in which they irritated or insulted you, they'll exchange the situation. They will ask you any other question in preference to respond to the hassle you posed. You don't confront a person you care approximately and assume this kind of retort, so it takes you off guard. Your train of idea is thrown off, and your mind spiral out of manipulate. Rather than worrying answers, your thoughts scrambles to discover ones to the query they requested.

This distraction technique is every different manipulative approach used by abusers to maintain you from forming coherent thoughts. The less centered and the more distracted you are, the an awful lot much less tough it turns into for them to put in force their narrative. You stroll right proper into a room with questions and accusations, prepared to confront them with their transgressions and abuse, and they hit you with a query that shakes yourself belief. You start to question your accusation, and in desire to being the first-class stressful solutions, you're the one on the lookout for to shield yourself and justify your movements.

Blame-Shifting

Rather than taking duty for his or her abuse, gaslighters shift the blame. When you confront them about one problem they stated or did, they will claim it changed into in reaction to something you stated or did first. They'll typically try to expose you the manner it's your fault, not theirs, and that their reactions have been justified. They twist the conversations and interactions amongst you simply so the blame usually falls on you, one way or the opportunity. It doesn't be counted what you're discussing, regardless of the fact that it have become your feelings and the manner they made you feel. They would probably however make it out to be that it have emerge as your fault and your terrible conduct brought about this whole mess.

"If you didn't do this, I wouldn't have dealt with you that way," is a very common respond used by abusers to justify their emotional abuse and manipulation. This rhetoric is robust and, sadly, quite powerful. After listening to it for a while, you start to accept as proper with that during case you behaved in every other manner, you wouldn't go through this shape of abuse at the same time as it's, in fact, now not your fault. No conduct warrants emotional abuse, but this isn't what your partner could have you ever ever recall.

Denial and Forgetting

For the gaslighter, it's all about escaping responsibility. If you present them with reality, they may deny it. They will observe some component and casually deny it in a while as though it in no manner befell. This first rate is infamous in abusers and emotional manipulators, and it's some thing you need to hold an eye out for. They will in no manner take possession of their movements and bad options. Instead, they will simply claim that this in no manner happened the manner you say it did. Needless to say, coping with some issue like this is past taxing and can leave you full of bitterness and frustration due to the fact you sense unseen and unheard. The individual you like the most has such whole dismiss on your terms and feelings that they deny what to your coronary coronary heart came about. This furthermore makes it an awful lot harder to move on and heal from the incident because it's now not resolved. It's just left there, placing, because of the truth your abuser stated they didn't do or say it.

Forgetfulness is every different weapon they use. If you gift them with easy evidence or get a person to corroborate your tale, your abuser can't flat out deny it. So, they claim they forgot. How are you able to punish someone for forgetting? They will play the sympathy card and blame you for scolding them over something they have no recollection of, and yet again we go returned to the blame-shifting cycle. If you appearance intently, you'll find out that this isn't simplest a one-time aspect in which they forgot a word they said or the manner they handled you. It's a sample. They abuse you, and whilst you confront them with evidence in their abuse, they say that they forgot approximately it or they didn't imply it. As a end result, your feelings aren't taken into consideration, and the pain stays due to the reality your companion denied all wrongdoing, whether or not or no longer via claiming forgetfulness or, even greater absurdly, claiming that it didn't even seem.

Taking Your Feelings Lightly

Sometimes, the abuser won't deny or say they forget about about an incident. They'll alternatively say that your reaction is blown out of percentage. They will assist you to apprehend which you're overreacting and trivialize your feelings. Rather than acknowledging your feelings and telling you which you're entitled to them, they'll mock and belittle them, taking the entire scenario as a right. "It have come to be simplest a shaggy dog tale, lighten up," they will say after mocking your weight at a residence party. They'll ask you to save you being so sensitive and to lighten up, which are all pink flags and sentences to be very cautious approximately as they could in no way come from a person who loves and cares approximately you. A man or woman who really cares approximately you may validate your emotions, not mock them.

Using Compassion

Gaslighters will constantly try to use compassionate terms and unique language to similarly misinform and control you. They will commonly try to clean matters over via the usage of phrases that they recognize may get to you. They'd say such things as, "You imply the sector to me, and I must in no way harm you want this." Or, "You apprehend how an entire lot I love you, I might in no manner perform a touch detail like this on reason." This shape of language isn't always actual and is best alleged to distort your belief of the fact, so you must 2d-wager the abuse that simply passed off. When you pay attention things like that, you begin to mellow and keep in mind that they may in reality such as you. If so, then possibly they didn't try this on motive.

A manipulator says all the terms you need to listen. When we're hurting, we want it to save you. We need to experience loved and to be reassured that what took place will now not stand up another time. You are in search of for comfort, and the gaslighter offers it to you in the ones phrases in choice to absolutely apologizing and taking ownership of what they did. The problem is, with on every occasion they repeat the identical behaviors that disillusioned you, their so-referred to as compassion lessens, and their terms are less enthusiastic. They simply say them because of the fact they have to, and on the off hazard that it'd get them off the hook.

Altering Facts

Last but not least, this approach is a few detail that every one gaslighters use, and it can have disastrous consequences ultimately. They will retell memories in a manner that makes them appearance pinnacle and makes you look awful, converting information in their decide upon. One of the maximum not unusual examples utilized by abusers is after they shove you towards a wall and afterward alter the story and say which you absolutely tripped, and that they have been trying to stop you from falling. There's a high-quality line among each actions, and deep down, that they were shoving you, but the manner they retell it later even as you're discussing it could turn out to be puzzling you. It's very easy to begin doubting your private reminiscences and your recollection of what befell. You'll convince yourself that you were wound up and surprisingly disturbing within the warmth of the combat, and perhaps your mind didn't method what sincerely happened. Planting this seed of doubt in your head is precisely what the gaslighter wants to do.

How Can I Tell If This Is Happening to Me?

The mind is a peculiar issue. You may additionally test those gaslighting techniques and don't forget dozens of conditions in which you professional this sort of behavior, and you continue to may not make sure that you're a sufferer of gaslighting. This is ordinary. After years of living dubious and confusion as to the kingdom of your private mind, it's predicted which you might be unsure whether or now not your partner or family member is gaslighting you. So, to assist with that confusion, permit's take a look at it from a selected attitude. Forget about the gaslighter's behavior for a minute. How are you feeling on this courting, whether or not or now not it's artwork, love, or family? Certain signs and signs will will let you apprehend if you're a victim of gaslighting so that you can gather that particular stop with out a shadow of a doubt.

Constantly Apologizing

One of the number one signs that you're in an abusive relationship with a gaslighter is whilst you discover your self continuously apologizing and blaming your self for the entirety. Whenever you attempt to look decrease once more and determine out why it modified into you who had apologized for a positive incident, it's commonly a haze. You hold in mind that it wasn't you who become at fault, but you're but the only apologizing. Gaslighters create an surroundings in which you commonly experience accountable, and also you continuously revel in that you need to apologize for who you are and what you do. They always turn the narrative and twist records simply so it's you who's responsible and chargeable for topics going incorrect, and so that you become apologizing. So, that is the number one signal you need to examine out for. Are you continuously announcing you're sorry, although it's not your fault? Do you usually apologize whilst your companion in no way does? A gaslighter will in no way apologize because it method they're guilty, which they'd by no means allow themselves to admit to being.

Feeling Inadequate

Picking up from the remaining problem, the abuser will make you revel in including you're in no way enough. Nothing you do is ever proper sufficient, and also you yourself are not appropriate enough as a person. This feeling of inadequacy is shared with the aid of manner of all sufferers of gaslighting who spend years being informed they may be no longer suited enough. One detail gaslighters do thoroughly is ready absurd expectancies, and while you fail to fulfill them, they make you enjoy including you're nugatory. You spend all your time seeking to stay as masses as their requirements when they themselves in no way do. They will permit you to recognise which you want to be more expertise, compassionate, and loving, at the identical time as they show none of these traits in the least. If you have got that feeling of inadequacy all of the time, and continuously struggle to grow to be a higher model of yourself due to the fact your accomplice goals it, you're in an emotionally abusive relationship with a gaslighter.

Self-Doubt

As described earlier, gaslighters try to make you continuously doubt yourself. This is why one of the maximum essential signs and symptoms you're being gaslighted is in case you discover yourself constantly doubting your mind and feelings. One day, you consider you're being abused, and also you question your accomplice's love for you. The next, you inform your self that it's involved in your head, and also you strive to influence your self that they're not treating you so poorly. You query your emotions, which no man or woman need to ever do. If you sense pain after an interplay with a person you need, your emotions are valid, and you shouldn't dismiss them. If you locate yourself doing that, some thing is wrong.

Moreover, you doubt not simply your feelings however additionally your notion of occasions and fact. When you're continuously being gaslighted, you start to have a hazy recollection of past sports. You remember their lies in desire to your model of sports. You don't take transport of as actual with your reminiscence any more, and it makes you indecisive and worrying all the time. You furthermore prevent expressing your emotions and mind because of the truth you don't trust them any greater. You comprehend that talking up will handiest make you revel in worse, so why trouble?

Asking Yourself If You Are as They Say

If you discover yourself asking if you're too touchy, you're in all likelihood in a courting with a gaslighter. This is one of the most commonplace strategies they use. They accuse you of being too touchy for objecting to their insults and abuse. It's how they invalidate and trivialize your emotions. They'll let you know which you're growing a large deal out of no longer anything to make you enjoy silly and silly for speakme. This manner, subsequent time, you received't take into account your perception and feelings, and also you'll select no longer to 'make a huge deal out of it.' Wondering in case you're too sensitive is a crimson flag which you must in no way neglect approximately about.

You might also additionally even discover yourself asking in case you're silly and dense, as they are saying, or if you're insane and emotionally risky. Your thoughts wouldn't stray off to the ones questions on its very personal, no longer till a person is pushing you there. You could probable pass as a long way as repeating those statements to yourself and insulting yourself on the same time as you do some element, in reality because of the reality a person keeps repeating them to you. No depend how strong you're, in case you listen sufficient insults each day from a person you care approximately, you'll ultimately begin thinking in the occasion that they're genuine.

You Don't Like Yourself Any Longer

Self-loathing is one of the worst aspect effects
of gaslighting. After spending some time
underneath the have an effect on of a
gaslighter, you discover that you now not
have this version of yourself masses. You're
irritated with who you're as someone and
what you've come to be. Worst of all, you
enjoy docile and passive, a shell of your
former self who have become robust and
assertive. You understand that you modified
into as quickly as more potent and higher,
however you can't undergo in mind a way to
go lower once more there or how you skip
thus far. Your insecurities get the better of
you, and you recognize it, making you
experience extra inclined and insecure. This is
exacerbated by means of using the reality
that you want to be careful what you're
saying or do spherical your companion simply
so they wouldn't go off on you.

You're Miserable

Living with someone isn't speculated to make you sad. Being in a courting want to no longer make you miserable. If it does, it can be due to the reality you're residing with an emotional abuser. When your companion gaslights you, this results in gut-wrenching feelings of loneliness and helplessness. Your buddies and cherished ones don't believe you, and they expect you're volatile and crazy even because of the lies your partner unfold. You feel all on my own and isolated with out a person to reveal to, and it's all their doing. Feeling powerless in a courting, no longer capable of trade its direction or walk away, generally results in excessive unhappiness and distress. It moreover leaves you with the constant feeling that some thing terrible is prepared to take vicinity. You're high quality it's coming, but you don't recognize at the same time as or perhaps what it's far. You genuinely apprehend that so long as you're spherical this man or woman, a few issue terrible is brewing.

The worst part of this distress you discover your self in is the truth that you're now not sure why it's taking place. You now and again feel it is probably related to your companion and their movements, but you're by no means certain. You recognize for a reality that you're sad, virtually not why. This misery and uncertainty mirror on other factors of your existence. You turn out to be no longer able to make selections because of the truth you don't bear in mind your self any more. Some sufferers of gaslighting ask their companions or special loved ones to make options for them actually to avoid in addition distress.

Hearing These Sentences

Gaslighters proportion a few common capabilities, like narcissism, which we'll speak in an upcoming bankruptcy, so they may be a bit predictable. If you still have a few lingering doubts about whether or no longer or not your associate is gaslighting you, those are some common topics you'll possibly pay attention them say manner too frequently.

• "You're being too touchy and blowing this out of percentage."

• "I didn't say/do that."

• "This by no means befell."

• "I don't hold in thoughts it that manner."

• "If you have got been paying interest, this wouldn't have passed off."

• "If you have been listening, we wouldn't be in this mess."

• "We went over this earlier than, can't you undergo in thoughts?"

• "I don't want to repeat myself, but I'll do it because you appear to miss."

• "You need to art work to your conversation capabilities."

• "This isn't nicely without a doubt worth all this. Calm down. Relax."

• "You're in reality too emotional."

• "Don't take topics so seriously."

• "You constantly try this and leap to conclusions."

• "I come to be joking. It's not my fault you may't take a funny story."

• "You need to be more thick-skinned."

• "I'm most effective announcing these items because of the fact I love you, and also you want to art work on your self."

• "No one has ever stated those subjects about me. You're the first-rate one I seem to have troubles like humans with."

• "I recognize you higher than you apprehend yourself, and I apprehend what you're thinking."

• "How can you believe you studied that?"

• "Can't you pay attention yourself pronouncing the ones topics?"

• "You always do that, and it makes me experience..."

• "You constantly say this..."

•"If you keep performing like this, you may lose me."

These are only a few examples of things gaslighters frequently say, and as you could see, they replicate the techniques we noted earlier that they use to control and manipulate you. Just because of the truth a person says this type of sentences doesn't mechanically imply they're gaslighters and emotional abusers, but in the event that they use some of those pretty often, then you need to be conscious of their conduct. Chances are, you'll phrase greater toxic patterns and terrible behavior that you disregarded in advance as ordinary.

In this chapter, we defined what gaslighting is and the way you can spot a gaslighter. Pay hobby to the signs and symptoms because they're there. You just need to famend them in place of burying your head in the sand. The more you start to understand that there may be a trouble, the better your probabilities of solving it and breaking loose to begin your recovery adventure.

Chapter 3: How Gaslighting Affects Your Life

Now that you recognize what gaslighting is and the manner it can take place to you, we'll dive similarly into the outcomes of gaslighting and the manner it can have an effect in your life in risky strategies. We already referred to some of the strategies it may have an impact in your highbrow u . S . A . And make you unhappy, and now we'll test greater consequences. You need to apprehend that you cannot constantly have those styles of issues proper now, however you in reality will in case you stick spherical extended sufficient with an emotional abuser. The human psyche is a frail aspect, and if it continues getting battered over the direction of a few years, the mental, bodily, and emotional damage may be devastating. The proper facts is, irrespective of the truth that, you can generally get better, no matter how an prolonged manner down that hollow you're. There is a mild at the prevent of the tunnel. You really need to apprehend what's being completed to you and the way it has modified you to get there.

Short Term

Frustration and Irritability

The results and dangers of gaslighting show up in each the quick and extended terms. The first trouble you may revel in brief-term is a horrible feeling of frustration. You're constantly preventing at the aspect of your associate, coworker, or family member, and they in no manner widely known their fault and the manner they harm you. Even worst, they normally make it out that it have turn out to be your fault even as you recognize for a fact that it wasn't.

Remember that abusers don't begin their emotional abuse certainly and aggressively. Gaslighting starts offevolved with diffused remarks and jokes, once in a while masked as trouble, just so they don't pressure you away in advance than they have full manipulate. As a quit end quit end result, you discover your self developing pissed off, but you could not however have the functionality to inform that it's due to their emotional abuse. You're certainly moody and bummed most of the time. You're greater irritable than you generally are, and you don't recognize the purpose. Your irritability is fashionable earlier than the whole thing. You get angry at the smallest topics and in conditions which you typically wouldn't get worked up over. It then progresses on your interactions with pals, circle of relatives, and coworkers.

Confusion

When you're notwithstanding the reality that in the early stages of experiencing gaslighting, your mind despite the fact that can't without a doubt manner it. You're surprised and careworn, and also you're not exactly tremendous what's happening. You start to inform your self that it may't absolutely have happened that manner. Your husband couldn't have referred to as you names and insulted you. Maybe you took the terms out of context or misinterpreted what he modified into pronouncing. You tell your self those devices due to the truth you're however in wonder that they occurred, and what makes the confusion and disbelief even larger is the fact that they made up with you after the incident. So, you tell your self that the incident didn't without a doubt rise up the way you imagined it, and it changed into in all likelihood milder.

This confusion is the begin of loads big issues down the street. It spreads like a illness to as a minimum one-of-a-type regions of your lifestyles, and you find out your self being reluctant approximately topics that typically come to you without problem. As greater time passes, your confusion great grows and worsens. The 2nd time they abuse or insult you, you still can't manner it, and your marvel stays there, and the cycle is going on till you ultimately snap out of it and recognize what shape of a courting you're in.

Guilt and Shame

As we said earlier, your abuser will commonly attempt to make it appear like your fault, which results in you feeling responsible. However, your guilt can also increase while you recognize which you're not recognition up for yourself. You pays attention hurtful terms hurled at you, and you may see your associate mocking you in front of others. When all is said and completed, on the identical time as gambling it for your head, shame gnaws at you for now not pronouncing some hassle. You'll wonder why you didn't react and truly stood there. Then even as you confront your partner, they'll gaslight you and make it look like you're too touchy, or they'll deny it or take any of the opportunity techniques we pointed out. You're truely left with guilt and disgrace. When all of it takes place all yet again, your emotions of guilt make bigger worse, and it starts offevolved to enjoy like there's a huge boulder in your chest.

Fear and Trauma

When you confront your accomplice or family member for the primary time, and they snap at you, after the wonder and wonder fade away, you're left with fear. You see a issue of them which you've by no means visible before, and it scares you. You chalk it as an lousy lot as pressure and input the abovementioned cycle of false impression and denial, however at the same time as it takes vicinity again and again, you begin to be aware the sample. This creates a worry indoors of you that you can't in fact get preserve of as real with this person and haven't any idea what they'll be able to doing. If they'll be capable of snap at you, shove you in opposition to a wall, or insult you in the front of friends or own family—after which deny or lie approximately it—who's aware about what else they will do?

Before you understand it, you'll be plagued with highbrow trauma that came out of nowhere. You recognize that you're living with an abuser - someone you're terrified of - and you can't carry out a touch element about it. This form of fear can be paralyzing and demanding. You also can moreover moreover moreover even keep in mind soliciting for a harm or leaving, however you're too scared to carry out a touch difficulty about it due to the reality you cannot bear in mind your abuser's response or response to you leaving, that may be a frightening detail to experience.

Aggression

Many sufferers of emotional abuse and gaslighting grow to be competitive due to the fact the years bypass via using. Their irritability grows worse, and they lash out, unleashing the anger and frustration cooped up internal. Your aggression isn't because of the fact you're a lousy character, but it's clearly a reaction to the abuse, a safety mechanism your mind advanced as a preemptive strike of sorts. Unfortunately, in marriages, this aggression can often be directed at the youngsters. When your husband is abusing you, and you may't do something superb about it, you lash out on the youngsters for no obvious motive. Then, in a while, on the equal time as you recognize what you've completed and the fact that they're harmless in all this, your disgrace and guilt are exponentially advanced. It's a vicious cycle that some of women discover themselves in.

Behavioral Changes

As a give up give up quit stop result of a majority of those feelings, your behavior modifications, sufferers of gaslighting and intellectual abuse frequently have low conceitedness, reflecting on all elements in their relationships. They avoid eye contact and turn out to be an entire lot a great deal less confrontational, no matter the reality that they need to, and need to be. They discover themselves frequently crying without a smooth reason – their our our our bodies' manner of liberating the mounting horrible emotions. They emerge as compliant and passive, and that they allow others boss them round, even though it come to be never who they were. You find yourself plagued with a normal feeling of defeat, and it affects the way you understand the arena and the humans in it.

You understand that you want to stroll on eggshells round your abusive associate, but you can't help but do the equal spherical exceptional people, too. You allow your coworkers promote off their obligations on you, and your boss abuse you, and it spreads on your relationships collectively together in conjunction with your pals and circle of relatives, too. The worst part of that is you are conscious which you're doing those gadgets. You see your self shying a long way from war and apprehend that others are strolling in some unspecified time in the future of you, and also you sense that there can be not some issue you may do about it. While this helplessness is without a doubt the worst aspect you may enjoy, there are subjects that you can do. You can find a manner out.

Physical Changes

Sadly, the adjustments you experience boom for your frame as well. Living in normal confusion, worry, shame, guilt, anger, and all the one of a kind emotions that accompany being gaslighted and emotionally abused in the long run effects in your body acting out. Victims of emotional abuse have trouble concentrating, and they emerge as without troubles distracted. They can be troubled with the useful resource of unexpected complications that they don't normally have. You might possibly start to experience nightmares and function hassle slumbering as strain, anxiety, and anger are emotions that could outcomes have an impact in your sleep cycle and stress you into insomnia, amongst one-of-a-kind sleep problems.

You may additionally furthermore moreover begin to revel in excessive blood stress and its associated problems. With every argument and each insult, your coronary coronary coronary coronary heart races, and your body reacts. Living in steady worry and frustration stresses your frame out and effects in muscle anxiety and stiff joints. The mind controls the frame. If your mind is constantly stressed and struggling, your body will undergo genuinely as a notable deal.

Long Term

Anxiety and Depression

In the long term, patients of gaslighting and emotional abuse be worried with the beneficial useful resource of excessive anxiety and despair. You emerge as agitated all of the time, and also you worry approximately the entirety. You worry that the waiter at the café can be rude to you in case you sit down too prolonged and order superb one drink. You surprise in case your coworker hates you and if your pals are unnecessarily suggest to you. Everything turns into distorted, and now not a few component goes without trouble any further. You can also fall proper into a rustic of scientific melancholy in which you're no longer satisfied or captivated with a few component. This interprets to the shortage of will to get away from bed in the morning or go away your own home. You revel in heavy in each the bodily and metaphorical revel in.

For a few sufferers of emotional abuse, growing suicidal dispositions is more than in all likelihood. They see it due to the truth the splendid manner out of their hell and the handiest to break out from their distress. Some researchers get keep of as real with that the despair and tension due to emotional abuse can result in critical ailments like fibromyalgia and continual fatigue syndrome.

Strained Relationships

One of the worst outcomes of emotional abuse and gaslighting is having strained social relationships collectively along side your circle of relatives, which takes place in masses of instances. Your abuser doesn't even need to try to isolate you all the time ultimately. They recognize that the adjustments on your character and conduct can be sufficient to electricity human beings away. Victims of emotional abuse are irritable, annoying, competitive, and indignant most of the time, that could placed a strain on any courting with any cherished ones. Some may additionally additionally additionally moreover feel which incorporates you're bringing them down, and your presence makes them aggravating. Even circle of relatives individuals need to likely have a few emotions of resentment in the path of you, specifically if your abuser has poisoned them over time with communicate of strategies insane and emotionally risky you are.

It takes effort and time to repair those relationships while you're in the end unfastened out of your abuser, and it's now not normally easy. This is why the effects of emotional abuse on social relationships can be disastrous and one of the worst outcomes of leaving an emotional abuser. Fortunately, some of your buddies and own family will show sympathetic and records once they see you going all all another time on your older self on the equal time as you go away your abuser.

Trust Problems

Old relationships aside, most survivors of emotional abuse battle to shape new and wholesome relationships. After spending a long term with an emotional abuser who lied and twisted information every day, it's now not surprising that you could have troubles trusting humans ever all another time, especially nearly approximately relationships. This lack of potential to honestly accept as real with drives a few humans away, and until you've decided a way to agree with all all all over again, you may emerge as with extra bitter feelings of loneliness and isolation. This is why specialists endorse treatment after breaking free from abusive humans so you can learn how to endure in thoughts over again.

Dependency

Abusers need you to be in reality counting on them. The greater based totally completely virtually truely you're, the more now not going it turns into that you can leave. When you may't endure in thoughts your lifestyles without them, it will become greater hard to head away, no matter what they do. As a impact, emotional abuse sufferers be by way of of the usage of dependency on others that could maintain after leaving the relationship. You are searching out for unique people's validation and approval because of the truth you could't provide them to yourself. You try to please others regardless of the reality that it comes at your very private price. The form of emotional instability that includes leaving an abusive relationships takes time to restore.

It's a slow device rebuilding yourself notion and conceitedness to a point in that you no longer want to are looking for others' approval.

This shape of unstable dependency now and again extends in your abuser. Victims broaden Stockholm Syndrome, because of this that they come to be bonded and in the route of the abuser and pick out out with them. It's your mind's strive at dealing with the abuse and making it prevent. This makes it a splendid deal more tough to transport away as you come to be too reliant at the abuser, and a few sufferers flow into as far as protecting their actions. You may find out your self justifying their movements to others who strive to help you go away. You'll tell them that an abuser is a remarkable man or woman deep down and that they're misunderstood. You'll make up excuses for them, all due to the fact you've end up too counting on them and might't recollect surviving with out them. The abuser attempts and every so often succeeds in growing the phantasm that you don't stand a risk to be had with out them. They'll convince you that the location is a horrible jungle that you cannot navigate without their assist, all to make you so counting on them which you couldn't probable do not forget leaving.

Addiction

Another unfortunate effect of emotional abuse is developing substance dependancy. Some sufferers can't address the miserable reality of dwelling with an abuser, and they take chemical substances to assist them get hold of and cope with this shape of dating. This substance abuse can spiral out of manage and bring about disastrous outcomes or lack of life in the long run. It doesn't begin with unlawful drugs constantly, but antidepressants and high-quality narcotics that might seem innocent if taken pretty. But with each fight and each gaslighting incident, your intellectual u.S. Worsens, and the narcotic becomes your most effective manner out.

The emotions of loneliness, melancholy, isolation, and helplessness that abusers nurture are devastating, and a few can't find out every extraordinary escape however narcotics. The abuser may additionally even recognize approximately this substance dependency and do now not a few issue. They also can furthermore hunch as little as the use of it to similarly smash your vanity and humiliate you. They'll will assist you to recognize that you shouldn't speak or object due to the fact you're an addict. If some aspect, abusers use substance dependancy as another device to in addition growth their manipulate in a courting.

The abuser's intention is to hold you on this abusive dating. They wouldn't care approximately any of these outcomes or all taking location to you. As prolonged as you're beneath their manipulate, that's the first rate detail they care about. They can also even welcome you displaying signs and symptoms and signs and symptoms and signs and symptoms and signs and symptoms and signs and symptoms and signs and symptoms and symptoms and signs of depression or physical susceptible difficulty, because it approach leaving can be loads greater difficult. Gaslighting may additionally moreover trade into bodily violence in a few unspecified time in the future or the opportunity in a dating, making topics worse than they already are.

These unlucky results of gaslighting increase over the years. You may not note them all at once, particularly at the start, however as greater time goes thru, you'll come to be more aware which you're converting. It's a terrible problem to experience changes to your thoughts and frame that you may't simply deliver an motive for or recognize. You clearly realize they're taking area, and also you experience helpless to prevent them. This is why leaving gaslighters and emotional abusers is vital and want to be carried out as rapid as possible.

Can Gaslighting Be Unintentional?

Before moving right now to the subsequent financial disaster, one more element simply well sincerely truly really worth discussing is whether or not or now not or not or now not or not or not gaslighting may be intentional. Is each emotional abuser a narcissistic manipulator with a pre-decided plan on how they will be capable of control you for the destiny years? Many are, but some aren't. Some people gaslight their partners or coworkers through the usage of way of threat. It also can additionally have the identical outcomes and result in the equal consequences, however their intentions might not be as malicious as a manipulator who is absolutely privy to what they're doing.

Different Perspectives

It may be feasible that someone who is gaslighting you has natural intentions, and that they're not looking for to abuse you. Sometimes, it's only a distinction in perspectives. This kind may be very not unusual in families, directed from parents to their youngsters, however moreover in place of job relationships. Whoever is doing it doesn't want to make you revel in insecure or insane, although it is able to in all likelihood stand up. They actually see the location in any other case, and they don't recognize how your mindset may be this outstanding. As a forestall give up end end result, they function it to you being too touchy or unreasonably searching out due to this and charge in which they don't exist.

You can tell your determine, companion, or pal about a few issue that harm you, and they could pay hobby clearly fantastic, but they don't attain your perspectives. To them, they're right, and also you're incorrect. They don't acquire the reality which you're particular, and that they want you to anticipate like they do, although it's surely no longer you. Their intentions is probably innocent, but the behavior can despite the truth that be pretty poisonous and may make you enjoy isolated and on my own. You're no longer really on my own to your mind-set, and also you're no longer insane, no matter what honestly absolutely everyone says. There are others which consist of you, however your parents or buddies don't pretty get that.

Unwillingness to Learn

Sometimes, people are so set in their strategies that they may't get preserve of that there can be some unique way and don't want to understand it. When you offer an motive to your element of view to them numerous instances, they may will let you recognize that they don't get it and it doesn't make feel. They're not trying to find to gaslight or manipulate you. They clearly can't understand because of the fact they're not inclined to. They don't want to area within the attempt to benefit a modern-day-day thoughts-set. Maybe it's because it scares them and due to the truth they worry the unknown. It can really be a completely scary concept to have a test that what you've concept for decades isn't always continually the pleasant truth. As a prevent end end result, someone thinking this way will gaslight you with out records it. Their conduct may be taxing to deal with, and it may negatively have an effect on the recipient, but their purpose is not malicious. Sometimes, humans understand and be privy to what they want to in location of what's certainly being stated.

Hiding Guilt

People once in a while via the use of way of danger gaslight to cowl their guilt about a few element. They will divert and change the scenario and make you question your belief no longer due to the fact they choice to govern and gain manipulate over you but due to the fact they need to cover some reality from you. This is a bit extra immoderate than the preceding examples due to the fact the individual has deceptive intentions. However, the ones intentions may not be approximately you. Perhaps they're in search of to stop you from coming across a few detail that might alternate the way you check them. Your husband need to have achieved some hassle he is not satisfied with at artwork, so he lies approximately it and deflects. He tells you that it's enthusiastic about your head and that you take into account this at the identical time as you tell them some component is wrong. Needless to say, that is irrespective of the reality that a completely unstable way to talk and outcomes in poisonous behavior, but the intentions within the lower back of it no longer being specially malicious.

The problem with unintentional gaslighters is they may now not advocate to abuse you emotionally, but inside the event that they preserve doing it, then it will become truly as intentional and malicious as an emotional abuser. You will confront them and tell them how their response and phrases made you revel in. You will ask them no longer to do it once more because it made you revel in uncomfortable, and you didn't apprehend having a person query your notion of reality or lie flat out on your face. If the individual keeps down the same road and repeats what harm you in the first area, they do it clearly information what it does to you. They're no longer usually emotional abusers, but they percent inside the same toxic conduct that would bring about the terrible effects we stated in advance. Whether they're your discern, friend, or accomplice, you want to make it clean to them that they're gaslighting you, and it feels hurtful. If they don't widely recognized your pain and certainly keep deflecting and lying about it, or call you sensitive and say you're overreacting, then this is probably a dating which you need to reconsider. Your highbrow nicely-being is extra critical than keeping a courting with someone who doesn't care enough to install an strive.

Chapter 4: Recovery From Narcissistic Abuse-The Fundamentals

That it is probably higher for you, you have been nice. In your thoughts, freedom modified right into a given. You were confident for your functionality to bear the pain. Why has it been the form of project? Why does it appear that the pain has taken up house in your coronary coronary heart and thoughts? You appear to be restricted hundreds greater than you have been before. The manner of getting higher from a narcissistic relationship also can range from that of other types of separation. Several instances can also make it loads extra difficult for you, this is why you would possibly experience in particular bereft in the months that comply with your departure. Learning approximately the motives why it is able to be hard may probable offer vital expertise which could help you in figuring out that each one of your terrible mind and feelings are brief—they'll be just the end result of the abuse you have got been subjected to for good-bye. The faster you recognize wherein they're coming from, the sooner you may be able to nip them within the bud and regularly loose your self from entanglements.

1.1 WHY IS HEALING SO DIFFICULT?

You've possibly needed to allow a person pass sooner or later in your life. Did you've got have been given a poisonous friend whose person sincerely did not mesh with yours? Did you've got an absentee companion who wasn't pretty what you had imagined them to be? Was your colleague a aggressive person who appeared every organization as a chance to "get beforehand?" Each of those instances might also moreover provide its very own set of issues, but one element is advantageous: Saying good-bye and taking walks away maximum in all likelihood did now not make you revel in sick in your stomach. As your coronary coronary heart and thoughts fought to reduce the very last of the links that certain you to this man or woman, it end up exceptional natural that you can have felt some residual consequences of the connection. However, after some days or even weeks, you had been maximum in all likelihood decrease again in your preceding diploma of functioning. Without a person else bringing them up, you may no longer have even had to think about that person the least bit! You recovered, you moved on, and also you have turn out to be more healthy as time went on. Why is it so tough now whilst it come to be this hard in advance than? It is the precise trends of a narcissistic dating that make it so tough to deal with.

In this case, it's far possible that you enjoy the

identical immoderate discomfort which you had after they have been part of your life. So, what exactly are the variables that make it a lot greater hard to collect achievement?

The Hold of the Narcissist

When it entails retaining their sufferers in line, the keep near is possibly the most complex and a achievement tactic a narcissist can use. Eventually, a metaphorical preserve is mounted over the years, built on a basis of conditional love and affection, and then carried out as a device to compel you to act within the way wherein they need. Once the sufferer has grown to much like the narcissist, the abuser will hire this attachment for their personal economic benefit. It is not uncommon for the victim to be used as a scapegoat for masses of issues within the narcissist's existence, despite the reality that the victim had no element inside the genesis of the state of affairs to hand.

The narcissist now believes which you are the supply of the hassle and that you are in rate for all the topics that skip incorrect for your joint existence. These human beings convince you which you need their services due to the reality you are not best and they realize what is exceptional to prevent you from inflicting extra damage on yourself or others. They aren't best each. They ingrain the belief that you are reliant on them, and that they make you feel as in case you owe them an explanation or apology for each little mishap that happens. In assessment, you've got come to phrases with the state of affairs. You are excessive nice that they've the best intentions due to the compas- sion, tenderness, and "love" that they showed you while your courting became honestly getting began. They've persuaded you that they're "advanced" to without a doubt everybody, even yourself, which makes them the handiest possible suggest and the pleasant person who can deliver you with confirmed reality and advice at this problem to your existence. You've unwittingly been trapped of their internet, and you have not any idea the way it took place. They make you experience relying on them, and the number one idea that entails mind whenever you want to make a choice is, "What would possibly they anticipate?" You're constantly strolling on eggshells, cautious to now not say or perform a touch component that would dissatisfied them, and seeking to do all you can to meet them, no matter how difficult the situa tion seems. The easy act of leaving, however, will no longer be enough to demolish such an entrenched tool.

You will lose your capacity to pick out in the long run, because of

this device's slow deprivation of your freedom. The abuser's dependency on you will become reflexive, and it will become more hard so that you ought to make picks for your self. So, now that you've lengthy long gone, you are probably questioning what you should do subsequent. When it entails the approach, you revel in the want to have a person direct you, and the most effective individual who includes thoughts is your abuser. Unfortunately, at this difficult time, no character else might be capable that will help you as hundreds as you may.

1. 2 ANXIETY AND GUILT ARE TWO EMOTIONS THAT MIGHT ARISE

In a narcissistic courting, there may be no such issue as a "civil disengagement." This manner that you and your abuser are most probable now not on speakme phrases. As a rely of reality, you will probable in no way be capable of communicate with them all over again. Accepting this as a fact of lifestyles is critical to transferring on. Recognizing which you are not on extremely good terms together with your abuser may additionally result in emotions of guilt. So, now that you're retaining off each special all of the time, you feel accountable about the us of your courting because you have got been persuaded that the whole lot wrong is your duty. If you enjoy guilty, you can try to climb once more into their modern-day day device and make an apology, further to name for your rightful characteristic. In the intervening time, going decrease again and apolo- gizing for some thing that wasn't your fault may want to do now not something to assist the state of affairs due to the fact you didn't do some thing incorrect to begin with.

Many sufferers of abuse end up rekindling their relation- ships with their abusers due to their emotions of guilt. This is why guilt is that this sort of extensive factor in failing rehabilitation. The easy act of allowing guilt to compel you to obtain out might be very risky as it offers the abuser with the danger to mound your mind and emotions, growing the hazard that you may experience abusive conduct another time.

Insufficiency of Support

It might be hundreds less difficult to live with narcissistic abuse in case your circle of relatives and pals ought to provide you with encouragement and expertise. However, due to the fact narcissists are masters at deception, they are able to keep their actual selves hidden from absolutely everyone and surely all and sundry of their lives. Although their proper lives are far from nice, they cultivate an photo of perfection and thoughts, building a personality worthy of admire and adoration. Other people aren't capable of recognize the fact because of this properly-constructed farce.

Approaching pals and circle of relatives folks who might be aware about your abuser will almost commonly result in a dull surrender because of the truth they are unlikely to simply accept what you are pronouncing. After all, they have observed out to appearance the narcissist as the right individual. As a end result, they will finish that the problems you are experiencing are most likely the stop end result of miscommunication. The majority of the time, convalescing from a narcissist's abuse should be completed on your very personal. Of course, there will constantly be useful resource groups and net equipment which you may in all likelihood use to hook up with others who have experienced comparable conditions. However, when you have been hoping to accumulate the help of others for your instantaneous area, specially if the ones people are also familiar with the narcissist, it might be tough to garner their compassion.

The Influence of Mainstream Media on Public Attitudes

They receive as actual with that love conquers the whole lot. The media has taught us masses at some level in the years. True love is probably found in literature, movies, and track, and it could correct any errors. We must be unselfish, die to ourselves, roll with the punches, and sacrifice our comfort and luxury to demonstrate our love for others. So, whether or not or no longer or now not it's miles a chum, a family member, or a love associate, the selection to keep stopping might be very effective because it's what we have were given been educated to do. We get our glad finishing, that's glorified inside the large majority of films and songs that we love in recent times. Unfortunately, there can be a form of sturdy love and devotion that the mainstream media fails to apprehend and have a good time, and that is self-love and self-reputation We are often labelled self-centered, inconsiderate, and selfish if we tell people that we did some thing out of a desire to be loved through ourselves. We're now not putting forth sufficient attempt, and we're actually too gradual to show humans affection. We do now not recognize the nicely nicely well worth of various human beings, and we do no longer see the charge of the lengthy-term connections we've built. But, earlier than you offer such thoughts any area to your head, keep in mind that you are the most important individual you understand. So, do now not permit anybody to discredit your efforts to attend to your self, specifically in case your abuser has completed no longer something to illustrate that they may be genuinely involved about your well-being. Many people had been conditioned to act like love-giving robots, able to shelling out love and compassion even in the maximum attempting of emotional conditions. However, you can not pour from an empty vessel, and you genuinely do now not need to enjoy responsible for a courting that you are surely seeking to shop. A relationship is a -manner road, and if excellent one person is clocking in at all of us moment, it will in no way education consultation. Putting your self first is not a selfish trouble; as an alternative, it's far a mature way of handling difficult situations. You can in reality contend with someone handiest if you have faith for your very personal potential to like, which starts offevolved collectively together along with your very personal self-assurance.

Furthermore, this form of powerful warranty in your being will appeal to the equal form of character, taking into consideration the improvement of a wholesome, flourishing relationship free of pretenses and hidden functions.

The Unaddressed Reality

Perhaps you've got been alerted to the indicators a while inside the beyond. Perhaps you have got already been aware about the uncommon behavior. Perhaps you made a decision to preserve your mouth near due to the fact you did no longer want to start a quarrel with someone. Perhaps you didn't observe because of the truth that wasn't the way you grew to understand them. Whatever the scenario might be, you've got been privy to the caution indicators and decided to brush aside them.

Numerous sufferers of narcissistic personality sickness are aware about the complex character prolonged in advance than it manifests itself in any shape or way. The fact is, they select out to stay silent and avoid war due to the reality they want to expect the splendid goes to take location. For them to assume that this is a pleasing person, they ought to obtain as proper with that those glimpses of unusual behavior are not some element extra than remoted incidences. Making a selection in competition in your instincts and in the end coming across which you have been correct for your emotions can also make it very difficult to go on. You'll discover that the emotion of having betrayed your radar may additionally make you need to conquer yourself up and weep over the milk that you've spilled for your very own carpet. No one is free from making errors. As devastating due to the fact the consequences of rejecting your gut instinct can also seem, in particular given the reality which you had been stuck inside the narcissist's grip, you have to recollect that the error served as a valuable mastering possibility for you. Not surely anybody is subjected to and survives such extreme abuse; consequently, you've got have been given an extraordinary possibility to enlarge and extend in a manner that many others do not. If something happens over which you haven't any manage, do not beat your self up about it.

As an possibility, appearance ahead to the future and discover ways to provide right understand on your gut instinct on every occasion it serves as a caution. Using your instinct to hold you consistent from various dangers to your environment might be a pleasant marvel. All it takes is a touch time and effort on your element.

Healing's Foundational Elements

Going through the way of healing is probably hard, specially at the same time as one is coping with narcissistic abuse, which has its very very very own set of problems. Although it is a difficult venture, there are strategies to make it a touch less hard. One of them is being acquainted with the basics of restoration. These foundations are meant to provide the statistics and perception you need to effectively decode your situation. If they may be in a feature, they need to be capable of assist people make revel in of your cutting-edge-day role as well recognise the truth in the back of the narcissist's behaviors and goals, among distinctive subjects.

Understanding the Narcissistic Personality in its Real World Applications

Some of you could have felt as though a slight bulb grew to turn out to be on on your thoughts while you first heard, have a have a look at, or found the word "narcissist." Wow, there can be a phrase for all of the abuse you have got been subjected to for a long time body! The event became very eye-setting up. When a call is located to a perpetrator's abuse, it is a breath of sparkling air for hundreds people who've been victimized by using the usage of this kind of character, as it confirms their plight. Although those human beings do exist, they are famous for attractive inside the equal form of sports activities sports as folks that have been achieved in opposition to you. In distinctive phrases, no matter the reality that anyone round you does no longer consider your tale, you enjoy fairly justified in what you're doing at this thing.

As future might have it, this revel in isn't always limited to a single event. Throughout your rehabilitation, you could get get proper of entry to to loads of records a awesome way to appear to you need "a-ha" moments. This will progressively display the fact about your situation and the truth of the character you believed you knew. While you are receiving treatment for your trouble, it's far pretty encouraged which you keep reading the narcissist archetype. By analyzing credible assets and reading approximately the psychology at the back of their concept strategies, you may be higher capable of placed all of the many contacts you have got had with them into context. The greater you understand, the less difficult it will become for you to break free from the feeling that you made a mistake through way of way of completing your dating. As you benefit a deeper information of their sports, you'll rapidly realise which you did not do some factor incorrect inside the first location and that all of the struggling, struggles, and uncertainties you've got been handling for years may be traced again to their poisonous man or woman.

Making Reminiscences of the Past

If you have got had a bad come upon together with your abuser, questioning returned on such memories may additionally feel like touching a heat iron. Some humans get fed on with the beneficial aid of them, leaving them with a unusual aggregate of want and guilt in their stomachs. If you're despite the fact that within the early ranges of your recovery, it is reasonable that you could need to avoid considering what happened for your beyond.

The data of narcissistic conduct will preserve to emerge from the depths of your mind, and you may be higher organized to place each reminiscence right into a greater great context. Only by using manner of reflecting on the beyond are you capable of recognize the reality of each state of affairs you have got were given encountered, that allows you that will help you see how their moves were interfering with your lifestyles. A little one includes comprehend that their mom's compulsive want to buy the most high-priced toys and apparel changed into not an expression of affection but, as an opportunity a manner of demonstrating her monetary independence to the a whole lot much less financially capable parents in her company. Some individuals study that their associate's choice to stress them to reject art work possibilities changed into not sincerely in their high-quality interests but, instead, modified right into a tactic to maintain manipulate and dominance in their courting. Though you will continuously be beneath the affect that the selections made with the useful resource of a narcissist were the top notch feasible ones, on the same time as you look once more with the brand new facts which you've received, you could recognize that nearly the whole thing, each the first-class and the awful, end up part of their intricate scheme to hold manage over you and preserve the ball in their hands. It is critical to keep your distance.

When measuring the distance among two places, there can be no greater effective tool. The preference to move again in time and make amends, similarly to the need to region this rupture inside the returned of you, might be continuous partners on your recuperation path, however you ought to chorus from doing so, no matter how an lousy lot it runs towards everything you receive as actual with in, irrespective of who instructs you to do it, and regardless of how a first rate deal it nags at your coronary coronary heart. There isn't someone extra worth of affection than you, and there may be clearly nobody a whole lot much less deserving of affection than a person who isn't always interested in your exceptional pursuits.

Your abuser could have sufficient white region to bring together a realistic image of fact in case you preserve your distance and refuse to interact with them. Instead of relying on that individual to enhance the strategies to your mind, you can put on them down and step by step however frequently placed the complete tool to a halt, ultimately liberating yourself from their manage and gaining a smooth perspective on who you're and what you deserve. When you're mistreated by way of the usage of a narcissist, only some individuals in your social circle who will apprehend what you are going thru. As a end end result, you will frequently pay attention the equal sentence time and again again: "People make mistakes; it's far nice trustworthy that you forgive them and supply them a second chance."

Narcissists are an exception to the norm. While it's miles real that humans make errors and that maximum of them deserve 2d possibilities, they may be an notable breed. They have no cause of converting, they don't have any records, and they may in no manner give up. If you want to restoration your relationship, you need to first take some time to mend it, which enhances the narcissist's perception in their very very personal unshakeable rightness. Ultimately, you need to renowned that reconciliation is out of the query on your scenario. You is probably pressured to spend the rest of your lifestyles without this a person in your circle of have an effect on. Although this might be a difficult pill to swallow, you need to recognize that it's far for the first-rate.

When you've got been professional to location others in advance than yourself your entire life, loving your self is probably hard. But each journey starts offevolved with the first step. Recognize that you want to preserve your attention in a few unspecified time inside the destiny of this method. Always hold your eyes and mind focused at the goal, and in no manner lose sight of why you're doing this in the first place. The finest version of your life awaits.

Chapter 5: The Narcissist Personality

Each individual is unique in their personal particular manner. Starting as early as primary college, we are taught this concept. When it have become first spoken, it come to be visible as not anything greater than a old skool little bit of truth: We are all specific, and as a cease result, we must exit of our way to understand each other for the arena to become a happier region for absolutely everyone. However, as we come to be vintage, we understand that the essential "reality" may not be an correct image of fact. A lot of humans behave inside the equal manner, and that is specially genuine within the case of narcissists. In addition to being "psychopathic," narcissists are frequently descended from narcissists, which reasons them to act further irrespective of their cultural, racial, or gender origins. Every one in every of them believes the same thing, and each surely one in all them uses the identical strategies to attack and defame humans in their on the spot vicinity. As a cease end end result, due to the fact they may be predictable, it has emerge as a lot less complex for professionals to select out their characteristics and turn out to be aware of them in a collection. During this level of your recuperation, you'll likely find your self asking questions about your abuser's traits. The capacity to understand their motivations and the reasons for numerous styles that they may have shown may probably assist you in forming a extra sensible picture of who they genuinely are.

In a comparable manner, becoming acquainted with the traits of narcissists enables reduce the probability of being mistreated once more.

Detecting the Subtle Manifestations of Narcissistic Personality

They disguise their sports activities sports, that's why they're difficult to stumble on. When you to begin with met your abuser, you may probably have assumed that they've been a version citizen who had the whole thing in their existence well prepared. This first have an effect on of perfection also can have forced you to preference to hold them close to, which also can have marked the start of your violent courting with them. Keeping their real impulses hidden allows them to draw more patients. Likely, the more admirable they are, the more the variety of folks that want to be in their top graces, providing them with enough narcissistic fuel to feed their ravenous egos.

Thus, it's miles in all likelihood that you'll pass over a number of the telltale signs of narcissism due to the fact they may be so obvious to you. To better apprehend narcissistic person dispositions, underneath are some of the maximum massive diffused signs:

Neither a single left out shot nor a single unnoticed possibility

Nowadays, finding someone who isn't lively on social media is like seeing a unicorn within the actual global. In this point in time, it's far nearly not possible to no longer employ as a minimum social networking networks, way to the quantity of ease and accessibility they offer. As you would anticipate, your everyday each day narcissist ought to seize the danger to reinforce their public photo and resource the illusion they have got worked so difficult to create. To be extra precise: In current-day years, researchers have placed an growth in the superiority of narcissistic inclinations, raising the possibility that there may be a hyperlink among social media and this conduct.

On the floor, social media skills as a marketplace in which a narcissist can also moreover sell himself or herself to others of their social circle. Fans' likes are the cash, and the extra of them they get, the greater quite snug they are with their revel in. To get the perfect reflected picture of themselves on social media, humans frequently lie about precise snap shots of themselves, modifying the context of the pictures and generating a more aesthetically suitable posting. Observe the social media profile of a narcissist and you're possibly to find three topics. For starters, they will now not have any bad pictures of themselves to deal with. Each and every picture wherein they seem can be drastically polished, ensuing in a huge variety of likes and remarks. In addition, you can have determined that they constantly enjoy best days. A lovely meal with own family, a romantic dinner with their great one of a type, a hen creating a track on their windowsill within the morning, or a few element else that would look like a scene from a Hallmark film is the issue of each post. In addition, they're likely to interact in "modest braggadocio" about some elements of their personal lives. For instance, one narcissistic mom shared a photograph of a breakfast unfold she had cooked, with the caption "Labored over a warm range to supply this delicious lunch for my son—the top resident of the backbone surgical operation department at his medical institution— who's coming over in recent times!" Naturally, the picture become alleged to be approximately the breakfast she had organized, but her caption discovered out that she changed into using the occasion to boast approximately a few different accomplishment. Many humans will positioned up pics of unique topics while subtly together with pix of different items to focus on their belongings.

In one instance, a girl took a shot of her newly manicured nails and uploaded it to her Instagram account with the aid of resting her palm on the steering wheel of her Audi. A social media presence that appears to be too extraordinary to be actual might possibly, in reality, be a narcissist's the front for the vicinity to see. Keeping your distance from them and refraining from taking part within the buzz thru withholding likes and feedback will make you plenty much less liable to their traps.

Resistance to Corrective Measures

Even even as they may be speakme to an professional, narcissists have an insatiable need to be proper, and they will visit any duration to make sure that they get the final phrase in any state of affairs. You might be conscious suggestions in their aversion to correction in small but consistent times in the beginning, although it won't be as large because it is probably in a while. Consider the following situation: Two buddies are debating in which to move for breakfast on Saturday morning. "We'll certainly visit that burger joint on East Avenue that is throughout the nook. It's typically brunch time for me after they open at 10 a.M."

"No, I undergo in mind they open at 8 a.M.," says the opportunity. "I go to this restaurant plenty. I'll in reality display you that they're open and we can be on our manner."

Once they achieve the eating place, they find out that it is closed. The hours of operation begin at 10 a.M., consistent with the signal published out of doors the constructing. "Well, I walked via the usage of right here the day prior to this and they had been open at spherical 8 a.M.," the narcissist explains, now not trying to be labelled incorrectly.

"Throughout the week, they need to have precise strolling hours." Though the be a part of up the door said that the ten a.M. Agenda modified into determined every day, the friend had no way of understanding whether or now not the store turned into open at eight a.M. The day earlier than due to the fact he become not within the network. The narcissist modified into merely inventing topics to keep away from being incorrect, and he ought to deduce this from the fact that the economic organisation is open on the same hours each day. However, even supposing they may be actually in the incorrect on all fronts, a narcissist will fight teeth and nail to be the only who has the final say. No rely how wrong they may be approximately a restaurant's taking walks hours, they will no longer go into reverse and will virtually in no way obtain defeat

Unmistakable Vocalizations That Want to Be Heard

You've possibly attempted to strike up a pleasant chat with someone who is a narcissist. A "communication" is something that happens very seldom. Because they will not assist you to unique your self, speakme with a narcissist may also seem greater like paying attention to one. Narcissists experience that they may be proper and superior due to the fact they have got an entrenched sense of correctness and superiority.

All that topics are their private beliefs and thoughts, and no individual else's. Regardless of the way intellectually strong their arguments is probably, contributions from clearly certainly all of us else are inferior and mistaken. Of direction, it's no longer some aspect a narcissist should ever apprehend, given the reality that they may not even widely recognized the existence of other contributions. One element you may have a look at approximately narcissists is that they have got a propensity to speak over and above others within the verbal exchange.

Even in normal conversation, they use the opportunity to say their dominance, giving others little possibility to speak out towards their moves. Thus, the speak is probably guided in a route that is beneficial to each activities' respective interests. So, it's miles no marvel that, regularly, whilst you are speaking to someone who's self-absorbed, the dialogue devolves right into a self-promotional monologue.

Need to Please and Flatter One's Fellow Man

It is this attractive excellent that attracts people to narcissists within the first place. Narcissists have a very precise manner of engaging unknowing sufferers into being their narcissistic supply. They are absolutely privy to their need to feed off the love and praise that others shower on them. During your relationship, they inspire you to take pleasure in your non-public narcissistic developments, which is probably inherent in really everybody, however the fact that in a much much less excessive shape. When we see this exceptional character, we are pressured to live near them simply so different humans will hyperlink us to this ideal person. We all had that teenage preference to be exceptional pals with the maximum famous teenager in school. It's the equal detail. As a stop end result of our affiliation with this excellent man or woman, we motive that a number of their perfect inclinations would possibly possibly become our personal traits.

Unfortunately, the narcissist is aware about your efforts, and they may gasoline your desire to grow to be like them. As a quit result, they deal with you as if you're an extension of them, complimenting your efforts, making you revel in critical, and presenting you with validation this is seldom given to others. Because of this, you revel in deserving and proud, and also you need more of this shape of popularity. You locate techniques to satisfy them, you do topics actually to make the narcissist happy, and also you determine to hold your feature as their right-hand individual. As time progresses, you could see that the majority of your movements and alternatives are primarily based mostly on their possibilities and dreams.

As fast as you find out which you have grow to be too engaged in receiving, you need to are looking for professional help. Do now not depend upon outside validation; rather, take a look at yourself. If anything, the most effective type of confirmation this is genuinely worth pursuing is your very personal non-public accomplishment. However suitable it might experience to gain approval from others, studying to genuinely take delivery of yourself and being content fabric with your area of expertise is an awful lot greater crucial than any reputation you get keep of from specific sources.

Either Way, I'm Doomed.

It is common for narcissists to simply accept as real with that they're deserving of the greatest that everybody has to offer, even though they'll be truly giving out spare coins.

People spherical them count on to be serviced, and they expect those spherical them to be willing to provide their assets and time at their beck and contact. Finding oneself the point of interest of a annoying narcissist ought to probable emerge as a double-edged sword. You also can, at the handiest hand, be requested to offer some thing that is bulky or really too big at the way to cope with. Not handing over what they may be requesting, however, will bring about rejection, rage, and separation from the connection. Do or do not—in each case, you're doomed. You'll be aware that there may be no such factor as a victory at the same time as dealing with a narcissist.

However, the idea of a lesser evil is some thing you may use for your advantage. Giving in to their wishes will handiest maintain you entangled in their complex internet of deception. Choosing to stroll away, as an alternative, will put off you from the internet, however with a few repercussions decided with the useful resource of the narcissist.

Characteristics of Narcissistic Individuals

The phrase "psychopath" is used to offer an cause of someone affected by a intellectual situation and manifesting aberrant or aggressive social conduct inside the direction of their treatment. They are visible as risky and violent, which allows them to inflict excessive emotional, intellectual, and, in some immoderate conditions, physical harm on others of their instantaneous surroundings. Even if the truth that your narcissistic abuser is a psychopath comes as a marvel to you, you must recognize this. Those who fall into this elegance be afflicted through excessive mental illnesses with origins that move decrease again to their infancy. So, it is hard to help a narcissist in their rehabilitation. Researchers have placed patterns in the behavior of those who are psychopathic or narcissistic, based totally mostly on in-depth research.

These developments are discovered in virtually all narcissists, and a whole lot of them showcase the same personalities, if to various ranges. Bear in mind that regardless of the truth that we all have narcissistic tendencies, not all and sundry well-known them to the quantity that they're categorised as a psychopath or sociopathic persona. Only while the ones sports activities bring about troubles in social functioning is the character deemed to be an entire-blown, malignant narcissist in entire pressure.

Gaslighting

She become on the mobile smartphone along with her brother, catching up on all of the small topics that have been occurring in each in their lives because of the reality that they'd ultimate spoken. She had presently celebrated her daughter's 0.33 birthday, and he or she or he or he modified into telling her brother approximately how her parenting fashion had changed considering her daughter modified into born. She knowledgeable him that spanking became no longer a manner of field in her and her husband's own family. They determined that it have become ineffectual and bad and that it surely induced their toddler to observe out of worry instead of respect. She received admiration from her brother, who pondered on the generally their mother had whipped them into form when they were little youngsters. "Well, are not we satisfied it in truth is over?" Gabby asked, laughing.

Gabby paid a visit to her mom day after today, taking her little daughter together with her. It changed into time for them to end up closer. "She's been performing so real presently! As despite the fact that she's all grown up and prepared to take on the region," Gabby's mom stated as she sat frivolously inside the front of the table and watched her granddaughter paint.

"In my dating at the side of her, I've been experimenting with a current parenting method. Spankings no longer serve any cause. As an possibility, we sit down down her down and try to offer an motive at the back of the scenario to her. The stage of comprehension she has is remarkable," Gabby said.

When her mom came over to assist her granddaughter collectively together with her coloring, she said lightly, "Exactly, it is how I punished you."

"Really, Mom?" Gabby exclaimed with a grin and a laugh. "You have no concept how rich I will be if I had a nickel for on every occasion, you struck me!"

Her mom shook her head, lifted her brows, and seemed her within the eyes. "I'm sorry, but you are incorrect. I in no way spanked you."

The word "gaslighting" comes from the 1944 movie Gaslight. A man or woman who engages on this workout, in particular a narcissist, is making an attempt to plant seeds of doubt within the mind of the exceptional being focused.

The way of gaslighting varies based totally at the situation, but the cause remains the same: to recreate the beyond a good way to save you earlier faults or errors from being introduced to public interest. Gabby had a fantastic reminiscence of her mom hitting her and her brothers in the instances described above. She had confirmed this information at the aspect of her brother over the phone, so she emerge as positive that it wasn't a few element she had concocted straight away. After seeing how well-behaved Gabby's granddaughter changed into, Gabby's mother decided out that Gabby's parenting method have emerge as powerful, and it have turn out to be smooth that slapping end up now not the handiest shape of toddler area. Gabby's mom favored to break up herself from that approach now that it were diagnosed as unneeded, unproductive, and perilous, and he or she changed into able to achieve this due to the net. To guard herself, she said that she had in no manner completed it, no matter the fact that Gabby and her brother vividly recalled that this have become how they were dealt with as youngsters. It's viable that gaslighting would possibly possibly appear harmless in this situation, and Gabby and her siblings will just dismiss it with the aid of claiming that Mom is growing older.

The workout of gaslighting, alternatively, would possibly set off excellent doubt or even result in a victim doubting their sanity in more severe times of narcissistic abuse. The employment of this method thru narcissistic humans to shield their photo, no longer only inside the gift but moreover in the beyond, is actually one in all their favored strategies. They identified the importance of being satisfactory in every location in their lives, and that they art work tough to avoid being stigmatized for mistakes that occurred years in the past. By gaslighting, they are capable of brush previous mistakes below the rug at the fee of a person else's sanity, it is a small fee to pay of their eyes.

Campaign of Discredit

Looking for a proof as to why people could possibly start to remove themselves from you whilst you terminate your relationship with an abusive narcissist? The abrupt loss of friends might be attributed to their smear advertising and marketing advertising and marketing campaign sports. Although smear campaigns are extra not unusual inside the political place, narcissists have been acknowledged to use comparable strategies. After a narcissist has been cut off from you, one detail will have been obvious to them— you're privy to their real character. The effect of this is that, if you make a decision to show the narcissist for what they honestly are — which might possibly or won't be in your time table — they is probably compelled to stand through the use of and watch as their properly-created photo burns to the ground. They are not prepared to take any chances at this element. So, what do they do in this situation? For the sake of staying one step earlier, they use smear campaigns. As a end result of the expertise they have got about you and your relationship, they'll take the initiative to the touch common friends and friends to find out why you and your accomplice have fallen out of communication.

This may want to probably encompass manipulating nice sports and facts to make you seem like a heinous man or woman. Note that a narcissist will not be glad with certainly maintaining some hurtful topics approximately you on the internet. The cause is to very well discredit you. Thus, they might be wonderful which you could have a difficult time persuading others to help your feature, no longer most effective due to the truth you may seem untrustworthy, however additionally due to the reality your buddies and connections may additionally need to most probably select to shun you absolutely.

A narcissist's slander advertising marketing marketing campaign may additionally leave you with no person else to reveal to for comfort besides your self. Certain rumors and gossip is probably so negative that they'll threaten your paintings and your personal relationships. Remember that they possibly did not care approximately you in the first place, so do no longer be startled in the event that they remodel into someone who's unrecognizable and start to unfold outright falsehoods approximately who you are and what you have carried out.

Abuse Via the use of a Third Party

Individuals are the maximum sizable useful aid that a narcissist will ever own. Others are attracted to them due to their beauty and seeming perfection, actually as you were drawn on your abuser while you first met them. The unlucky reality is that each person who tries to get inside the manner of a narcissist will discover himself or herself managing an assault from their whole employer of fans. The term "abuse thru proxy" might be used to give an explanation for this. A narcissist's dissatisfaction triggers the commencement of the manner. When their choice to humiliate and discourage you takes maintain of them, they will do all they are able to to make you understand how upset they are in what you've got achieved. However, they will regularly pass the extra mile to make sure that they strike you in which it hurts the most.

The people who artwork for them are responsible for this. A narcissist will unfold terrible records about you to other people to your social circle, which includes your pals. Their goal is to influence these humans that you have devoted a severe offence and which you need to be punished extensively. Interestingly, they'll be no longer constantly drawing near with such sincere commands. The approach is more carefully associated with brainwashing, in that it consists of convincing others to definitely be given particular falsehoods and encouraging them to act on those ideals without immediately educating them. Consider the subsequent situation: Hannah is the youngest of 3 children. All of her siblings are A+ college students, bringing home amazingly first rate file playing cards and garnering a extremely good deal of wonderful remarks from their teachers. Hannah, as an alternative, is a under-common performer academically. Yet, at the same time as she does now not obtain the same degrees of achievement as her brothers and sisters, she does get respectable marks from her instructors. When she receives home from college with a failing take a look at, her father loses his cool and walks away. Her father reprimands her, accuses her of being unproductive, and expresses venture about her destiny.

He argues that her overall performance will not get her everywhere in existence, and he's sad on the opportunity of her not being able to accomplish as masses as her brothers and sisters have. Hannah is escorted out of dinner after being punished within the the front of her entire family. Then she retires to her room, wherein she sobs and sulks for the the rest of the midnight. Meanwhile, her siblings live seated at the table, and their father keeps to lecture them on numerous topics. He expresses his appreciation for everyone's try and willpower. He works tough hours to fund their schooling, and their grades replicate this. The kids have a warm connect- ment to

131

their father, and that they specific their appreciation for the whole lot that he does to ensure that they may be able to give you the cash for a notable training. During the conversation, he refers to Hannah as an ungrateful toddler, claiming that she is not enti- tled to the equal opportunities as her siblings due to the fact she does no longer respect what he offers. He advises them to now not have interaction with human beings like Hannah due to the reality they'll come to be a damaging have an effect on, most important them to lose sight of what's vital in life. Before concluding his speech, he states that he has no choice however to preserve walking hard and desire for the remarkable, notwithstanding the truth that a number of his colleagues do not apprehend what he has carried out. Following the perception of the discussion, all the kids go back to their respective rooms. As Hannah gets far from bed the subsequent morning to go to breakfast, she discovers that all of the meals has been ate up. Unapologetic, her brother informs her that she wakened too overdue and that now not some thing is left.

The equal harsh, unpleasant mind-set emanates from her siblings within the path of the day, and she or he feels as despite the fact that they may be doing their wonderful to avoid her organisation. As a cease result, Hannah feels on my own and embarrassed approximately her movements. She apologizes profusely to her father, saying she have been ungrateful for all of his tough artwork. However, he accepts the apology handiest after showing a palpable coldness toward his daughter in the following days, which the relaxation of his kids imitate. Identify the flaw in this case and provide an purpose of it to me. To begin, we need to renowned the purported aggra- vation of the conditions. To collect such remedy from her father and, in the long run, the rest of her circle of relatives, Hannah want to offer an motive in the back of what she did. An unsatisfactory grade (to be honest, a single failing grade) isn't always typically sufficient of a motive to be indignant. She could have been given a mild reminder to do better subsequent time. However, due to his individual tendencies, Hannah's father views failure as requiring a complete rejection of his daughter. As an extension of himself, his kids are unacceptable after they appear shortcomings, as those mirror adversely on him. Hannah changed into reprimanded within the the the front of the entire family, which tested his displeasure with her.

The truth that everybody else is there to pay attention and word her on the receiving surrender of the scolding not most effective draws interest to his rage, but also reasons her to experience embarrassed. Hannah's father then chats along together with his one of a kind kids approximately the scenario. He starts offevolved offevolved through the use of expressing his admiration and deal with them, telling them that he is thrilled with all the attempt they've placed forth to grow to be pinnacle college university students of their respective training. Without a doubt, we are in a position to deduce that the youngsters perform best due to their father's strain and not because of a proper desire to do terrific in their lives. When he speaks to the rest of his kids, he can now convince them to harbor unwell will in opposition to their sibling who, in reality, has completed now not whatever incorrect to everybody inside the own family. They don't have any purpose to be indignant collectively together with her due to the fact their problems are unrelated to her educational performance. However, because of the father's approach of department and conquest, they experience one with him and, hence, vow their loyalty through mirroring the emotions that he's experiencing. As a stop result, they emotionally abuse Hannah with the aid of manner of being bloodless and disdainful in the course of her. They forget about her and keep a region between themselves and her, treating her as although she were a pariah in her own family. In the cease, what occurred modified into this: As a end result of her "blunders," Hannah have come to be obligated to apologize, notwithstanding the fact that she had no valid purpose to acquire this. As a quit result, managing abuse through proxy is probably exceptionally difficult, as the victim is left feeling totally isolated from the state of affairs.

People who've professional abuse normally normally have a tendency to doubt their personal actions and occasionally count on that the abuser had a valid purpose for treating them badly. Additional strain from an "angry crowd" adds to the problem of waging a a success inner warfare. "If everybody is disillusioned with me, it have to be because of the fact I've finished some element very incorrect." Keep in mind that genuinely because a majority thinks some element, this doesn't suggest they're accurate in all cases. The experience of being on the receiving forestall of abuse thru proxy can also additionally reason you to doubt your integrity and validity; despite the fact that, being sturdy and deciding on to just accept as actual with the truth allow you to end up an awful lot a whole lot much less impacted through their rejection and combined abuse in the destiny.

Manipulation

Narcissists use such quite a few awesome manipulation techniques that it'd take a whole ebook to cowl all of them. We need to, however, talk the most everyday techniques they use, to offer you a clearer keep close in their real character. The first, and possibly most customarily implemented, is humiliation. Both non-public and public humiliation are meant to perform a dual purpose. It is their purpose to boom their enjoy of cost, grandeur, and mind and to make you revel in not as appropriate as them. Shaming you in the front of others, whether in public or in private, will encourage you to surrender your self to the abuser. "It is in my tremendous hobby to check from those who are greater informed than I am if you want to subsequently be definitely well worth of their admiration." As long as you have got this mind-set, all your moves and picks may be centered at the leisure and approval of your abuser, it honestly is exactly what they meant within the first region.

Narcissists also can moreover try to manage their deliver thru portraying themselves as patients. This is normally initiated whilst the abuser is placed in a situation in which they experience inconvenienced via the narcissist's goals, collectively with even as using. Consider the subsequent situation: Because Claire emerge as laid off from her interest while her organisation went bankrupt, she is jogging quick on price variety. Now that she has been out of labor for three months, she is starting off a name to her social circle for economic help. Her technique to Timothy for assist has been ongoing for lots weeks. Initially, he become greater than satisfied to provide some thing assistance he have to.

Claire's economic requirements, but, are starting to place a vital dent in his monetary organization account's bottom line. Once all over again, Claire goes as a good buy as Timothy and asks for coins, but this time her buddy isn't quite so accommodating. "If I spend any of the cash I surely have handy for a few factor else, I'm going to get at the back of on my bills. Clare, I choice you apprehend."

"I can't agree with this. I don't have a hobby, and I'm depending on this cash to make it through. The fact that you are 'behind' to your payments, instead, is notably more vital than my worries. Thank you for your time, and please take delivery of my apologies."

After the whole thing is said and completed, Timothy involves a selection to offer her the cash and makes a clean strength of will to pay his expenses together collectively along with his next sales.

Was Claire correct in her expectations of her friend? Plus, Tim is liable for his very non-public economic properly-being. If any man or woman works difficult for his money, he should have the freedom to decide the way to spend it. The choice to assist Claire is, consequently, in reality as an lousy lot as him, and nobody ought for you to keep his decisions in opposition to him.

To start with, it's miles essential to examine that Claire has been out of tough paintings for extra than three months, which shows that she may additionally have had greater than enough time to find a new role that could allow her to fulfil her economic responsibilities. The reality that she remains reliant on others to make ends meet suggests that she might be content material fabric material with the modern-day-day scenario of being able to stay on while not having to artwork for her residing expenses. However, however all this, she is a success in convincing Timothy to place her pursuits in advance of his non-public with the resource of creating him enjoy terrible approximately himself. To make it seem like Timothy is being unreasonable and grasping, she plays the victim, draws interest to her very very own problems, and downplays Timothy's difficulties. Narcissists frequently use conditional love as some other tactic of their armory. Acute narcissism elements the sufferer with simply the quantity of affection they need to hold them on the narcissist's correct factor, letting them sense worth and ok within the meantime. When a victim pleases them or does something to advantage them, narcissists frequently use this technique, which serves as first-rate reinforcement, encouraging the victim to preserve to do proper. However, proper love need to now not should be forced onto everybody.

Thus, love does no longer choose out whilst to be shown; it is expressed regardless of the man or woman's imperfections. A narcissist, however, isn't always able to engaging in the form of project.

As soon as their sufferer does some thing that is going toward their dreams, opportunities, or perspectives, the narcissist will without a doubt refuse to expose love and affection, making the sufferer feel worthless and now not worthy of the narcissist's interest. The narcissist will "forgive" the victim simplest after receiving an apology and reputation in their fault. The narcissist efficaciously maintains manage over the sufferer by using controlling whilst and what kind of affection is given. Getting on a narcissist's incorrect facet is in no manner an first rate idea, specially considering that their reward is alternatively prized. The very last point to make is that you need to be privy to the opportunity of being held accountable for the entirety by using a narcissist. This approach lets in them to maintain a smooth and blemish-unfastened public picture while concurrently using their victim to feel a revel in of responsibility for his or her movements. As a prevent quit end result, abusers take advantage of each chance to be had to them to keep away from being blamed for any terrible publicity that could stop end result from their conduct.

They want to find a victim—often their present victim—and flip each and each scenario spherical to make that character feel horrible approximately himself or herself. Thus, the victim feels unworthy and clings even greater to the abuser out of fear of being abandoned. A outstanding deal of the time, narcissists may even inform others about the victim's shortcomings. In this case, the scapegoat is well conscious that other human beings in their orbit are aware about their "errors," and that is completed explicitly. In addition to instilling disgrace, the victim is forced to publish absolutely to the abuser in case you need to reveal regret and a willpower to right their wrongs. These manipulation techniques not best reason the victim to reply in a specific manner right now, but moreover implant an extended-term mechanism that sustains the relationship in its contemporary-day state for an indefinite period. Victims who have their unfastened will and feeling of self- properly truely really worth taken away end up relying on the abuser, who would in all likelihood make use of this dependence to exert control over their mind and conduct. Is it simply essential to be on pinnacle of things? Narcissists live on adulation and reward, and that is why they are so a hit. They may also furthermore have a ordinary supply of narcissistic fabric in their ownership so long as they have you ever ever under their manage. The victim's insatiable want to satisfaction and placate the narcissist presents the abuser with a dependable deliver of adoration. Furthermore, they believe that their supremacy offers them the right to subordinate others. According to their ideals, they are the top notch, and as a cease result, they've got the proper to degrade and subjugate others in any way they see in shape. Due to their perception that they'll be extra informed than everybody else, they assume they will be doing you a decide on with the aid of taking rate of your existence.

How to Spot a Narcissist within the Real World

Are you having hassle identifying a person who is probably a narcissist or a sociopath? As a bring about their capacity in concealing their fact, they might be hard to discover. For some time, they're probably to seem best and well-rounded, to be able to reason humans of their without delay vicinity to attract closer to them. Only as quickly as you've got fallen too a ways into their lure do you recognize what they without a doubt are. It is possible to apprehend them within the actual international with the useful resource of a few terrific tendencies. The narcissist's inform-story symptoms frequently appear suddenly, supporting you to find out them with greater truth. Personality this is amusing to be round

Narcissistic people have an uncanny ability to provide themselves in a best manner to others.

A thrilled, smiling face and charming demeanor greet web web page web page site visitors, permitting them to revel in comfortable of their welcoming and pleasant surroundings. They will be inclined to make you experience suitable about your self, which may in all likelihood lead you to bear in mind that they actually together with you as properly. Speaking approximately their maximum prestigious achievements will carry attention to themselves, on the way to probably make you feel even greater comfortable in their corporation. In addition to being awesome and finished, this individual seems even extra deserving of admiration. Essentially, their complete demeanor evokes you to need to be their pal, to be near to them, and to be associated with them in any way you may. This is because of our natural choice to truly take delivery of as proper with that interacting with wealthy, smart, suitable, or "best" human beings can by hook or by crook boom our personal image. So, it is understandable that hundreds people located it tough to mingle with the maximum famous university university college students at our respective faculties. Consider their demeanor further in your stage of familiarity with them at the identical time as on the lookout for to apprehend narcissists. Any unpleasant statistics concerning who they may be has been observed out to date. Is it capability that you've heard recollections of a person who has accomplished or said some problem you do now not like? Or are they flawlessly polished and with out blemishes and imperfections? Be careful of folks who appear to be too brilliant to be actual; most usually, they will be.

Just one time it's miles required is even as it is important. When it involves the narcissist's mentality, there are various "stages" of fee. Narcissists trust that the ones who've obvious blessings, at the side of more money, extra expert accomplishments, or physical splendor, are advanced. As a end end result, those human beings get the most favorable treatment. People who share the identical stage of wealth, success, and splendor are seen as equals and are handled as such. When someone's self-worth is especially lower than the narcissist's, they're though entitled to praise and great treatment, but the ones are given to them first-class beneath advantageous conditions. These individuals need to do some thing to earn the approval and admiration in their narcissistic advanced. There are different individuals who are honestly dull to the narcissist. Narcissists will not trouble to be type to them or located forth any attempt to illustrate their notable competencies, as they may be considered vain and unimportant. Example: If the barista at their desired coffee shop makes the error of including cream to their order, the victim may also additionally react violently and unfairly. While on the grocery save, the narcissist may additionally criticize the cashier for spending too much time inspecting the matters in their basket, labelling her "lazy" or "stupid." If they're not able to deliver a solution in a well timed manner, they might offend the client care representative on the opposite give up of the choice.

Whenever it entails fulfilling others and gaining acclaim, a narcissist will located forth satisfactory the strive critical to placate individuals who they understand will usually be in their circle of contacts. Why ought to you spend power on prevailing the affections of a person you're not likely to look all over again? So, despite the fact that that is their first interaction with a narcissist, many menial employees undergo the brunt of their terrible mind-set. Is it viable to be by myself with a narcissist on the same time as nobody is looking? Prepare to pay attention some juicy rumors about parents to your social circle that you may not need to pay attention. It is the destruction of various human beings's image that narcissists are most captivated with. The act of speaking adversely approximately exquisite humans elevates a narcissist's shallowness, helping them to further refine their photograph, particularly whilst they will be in assessment to the individual being discussed. On top of all that, spouting disparaging remarks about particular human beings enables them reinforce their bonds with essential people in their narcissistic supply network. Consider the following scenario: At a celebration thrown with the resource of using a mutual acquaintance, Chris met Sheryl, who at once struck him as a captivating more youthful girl.

Aside from being clever and a laugh, Sheryl come to be capable of conducting an exciting communication with out being tedious. Plus, she become very appealing.

Chris became positive she have emerge as a dream, so he went in advance and requested for her cellular telephone sizable variety in advance than announcing good-bye that night time time. He approached Sheryl the subsequent week and asked if she'd like to meet up for a cup of espresso, which she simply agreed to do. They conversed for a while and have come to be acquainted right away notwithstanding the constrained time that they had to be had. Eventually, their dates have turn out to be a regular characteristic in their weekly schedules. It failed to take prolonged for them to get familiar with each one in every of a type to the component that Sheryl felt comfortable talking to Chris approximately extra intimate topics, and Chris felt the identical manner. Consequently, at the equal time as Sheryl inquired about his in advance romantic relationships, he did not maintain again. During her research, Sheryl positioned that Chris had been courting Tara, a college roommate, for approximately a month round years previous to her discovery. As a stop result, Sheryl took advantage of the situation to offer some records approximately the lady underneath the basis of simply being sincere and apparent about the individuals they each knew. Tara, she stated, have become promiscuous and taken guys into their shared region hundreds too regularly for Chris' consolation. She additionally said that Tara had an ugly mood, which prompted her to hurl devices approximately whilst she become enraged. Tara denied this.

Chris expressed his gratitude for having met Sheryl and expressed his alleviation that his courting with Tara did no longer keep. To the factor of comparing her with Tara, he stated Sheryl become drastically extra appropriate and appealing in hundreds of strategies, and that she became a protracted way greater appropriate in desired. Unfortunately for

Chris, most of the statistics that Sheryl determined out about Tara modified into based totally mostly on a few isolated incidents that did not correctly replicate Tara's massive person or attitude. On pinnacle of that, Sheryl felt it essential to speak poorly approximately Tara if you want to dissuade Chris from persevering with to find out her attractive—a perception that endangered Sheryl's feeling of superiority within the eyes of the area. Sheryl damaged Tara's reputation due to the reality she did now not want Chris to have even the slightest inkling that she might have been a functionality partner. When it entails speaking about unique human beings on your circle and the topics that might painting them in a horrible mild, you may discover that a narcissist has a outstanding deal of self-self notion.

In different times, you will possibly even experience as though the chats are wrong and invasive, mainly at the same time as narcissists are inclined to reveal such personal facts with someone they've just met a brief time earlier than.

Exaggerated but a success

A top notch success tale is one that everyone enjoys listening to about and discussing. That type of success, which encompass developing above one's times, beating the probabilities, and building a nice existence irrespective of being dealt a awful hand, is what motivates others to do their exceptional as well. Often, narcissists are the proper example of "rags to riches" memories, as the majority of them move straight away to achieve tremendous achievement of their careers because of their unquenchable need to enhance their recognition. The narcissist will no matter the reality that exaggerate their accomplishments. In extraordinary terms, they may exaggerate reality to appear more a success than they honestly are. Although they is probably in a better feature than the majority of humans, their real achievements might be plenty a good deal a lot less surprising than they make them seem. Investigate what this potential narcissist has to mention about their artwork, economic scenario, and beyond achievements in greater element. How realistic are they of their depiction of fact? Do they appear to be exaggerating the reality to raise their recognition as worthy of reward and admiration? It might be difficult to apprehend the fact of a narcissist inside the beginning because of the reality they seem like so charming. These outstanding pretenders recognize the not unusual choice that maximum people have for approval and validation, and that they understand truly what to provide to make you maintain to them, further to what to do to strike you in which it hurts the maximum. Taking motion and slicing the hyperlinks you used to have with the narcissist may thoroughly be the awesome factor you may ever do for your self on this lifetime, however there can be extra to restoration than leaving the scenario. According to what you've got genuinely found out to this point, the recovery method is significantly greater intricate than it regarded in the starting.

Chapter 6: What Caused Them To Exist?

They are unable to exchange. You should accept this as an unavoidable a part of your lifestyles scenario. These humans have intellectual trauma that has been profoundly ingrained in them because of years of mistreatment. Even inside the event that they favored to, it'd be tough for them to exchange their techniques. You might be thinking how narcissists came to be, for the reason that they may be so acquainted. Beginning in early infancy, it's miles a prolonged and tough device that have to be continued.

Narcissistic Parents

The urge for reward might be determined within the majority of people, if not all people. Some of what we do and strive for in phrases of achievement and prestige is probably stimulated through the opportunity of gaining repute and interest because of what we do and strive for. Of route, if we do now not allow our need for adoration to get the higher human beings, it might be justified as an incentive for us. As a end stop end result, you may argue that we all have narcissistic dispositions, despite the fact that they may be no longer completely manifested. These dispositions are heightened and emphasized specially conditions, causing the person to go into a nation of thoughts driven usually by using way of the want for recognition and reward. Internal and outside impacts coerce a person into motion to get interest and confirmation. This turns into their crucial kingdom of recognition. Early early life is a commonplace time for this to get up.

A commonplace trait among narcissistic people's mother and father is that they're themselves narcissistic. In their eyes, their children are an extension of themselves, and that they want them to try to be the best amongst their classmates for you to "deserve" the affection and approval in their households. When you assessment this with the manner a determine need to truly be, it's far easy wherein the hassle is. A little one's need for romance and affection from their dad and mom stems from the truth that the ones elements have a large have an impact on on their intellectual, emotional, and intellectual development. The trouble is that, because narcissistic parents bear in mind that their kids want to earn love and affection, they compel their children to take part in an economic device wherein their well well worth is determined by means of manner of the degree to which they fulfill their parents' desires.

One mother, as an instance, might forget about about and belittle her daughter because of the reality she wasn't excelling in university, regardless of the reality that she changed into returning home with a fairly super grade factor not unusual (GPA). Often, she should belittle her daughter and make amusing of her for being one-of-a-kind from her siblings, making her experience like an outsider in her non-public home. To avoid being labelled the "black sheep," the daughter labored very difficult in order to get higher grades in school, prompting her mother to wash her with love and adoration. Unexpectedly, she was informed that she grow to be notably superior to everybody else and that her mom had constantly suspected that she had the important abilities. At this level, the teen is aware of that the rewards of putting forth attempt in college and returning home with excessive marks have doubled. In the primary area, it allows her to win the love and devotion of her mom, which she appreciably wishes. In addition, she might be taken into consideration advanced to anyone else at university because of her accomplishments. That idea grows in power within the daughter's thoughts the greater she hears her mother repeat it. To win her mom's want, she have to keep to artwork tough even as moreover putting in herself because the superior individual in beauty, a role she merits.

Throughout her childhood and young adults, she keeps to exercise this conduct and contain it into all components of her life. The female is also taught the way to act within the the front of others, apart from the conditional love and hobby she gets from her mom. She is clothed and groomed with the exceptional care and hobby to detail, and her mother makes fantastic that she sticks out within the most flattering way. In public, the daughter observes her mom and takes notes on how she want to act. Consequently, she learns a way to located on a first rate display by seeming to be interested in others and turning into a extremely good conversationalist in order that others who see her and her family in public keep in mind they're a picture-best own family. This corresponds to the mother's preference to be praised and desired for the "lovely" own family she has created, and it strengthens the perception of "us toward them." On its most clean degree, this belief is favored via a narcissist, who encourages her children to behave in a selected way in order for them to enjoy the feeling of elitism she has created for them. Their potential to gather the concept of being a higher breed grows in electricity as they gain popularity from others in their at once environment. As they advantage reputation from those of their nearby location, their ability to accumulate the notion of being a advanced breed will growth.

A Misguided Approach to the Study of the Universe

Children who've been uncovered to this sort of conditional affection at some stage in their teens from a number of the most large people of their lives could in all likelihood increase defective vision with which to look the region spherical them.

It is feasible that the remedy they experienced as kids have to encourage them to try for greatness due to the reality their parents predicted them to gather greatness on the manner to be installed via the only-of-a-type organization of elites that their family claimed to be. With the adulthood of an man or woman, this individual could probable enjoy more integrated into the family shape. Consequently, they will be willing to expect that they have the authority to degrade others due to the reality they'll be a member of a own family that is superior, based totally totally on their parents' assertions of superiority. In this sense, you'll in all likelihood presume that there is not something to be sorry for whilst handling a narcissist, except for the unpleasant fact of having been unfortunate enough to fall into considered one of their webs. Their actions are surely unremorseful, and they may be unable to sympathize with you due to the fact they trust that they may be in fact sporting out their moral responsibilities to others. This organisation of people believes that their increased social popularity justifies their behavior. Because you're far lots much less in a function than they will be, you owe them for all of the help they've got furnished to you as a manner to at least get on their diploma. Right? Outsiders offer the gas for the fireplace. A narcissist may appear to be the entirety you ever preferred to be: sensible, extraordinary, a success, and financially strong. But this is actual most effective from the outside looking in. Those who're on the excellent element of these people promote the parable, making it appear as even though it's miles a reality for all people fortunate sufficient to be on their specific component. Don't revel in responsible or humiliated about believing that your abuser have come to be the perfect individual while you first met them. Most folks that come into contact at the side of your abuser experience precisely the equal manner. They become the focus of hobby due to their attractive air of thriller and extremely good persona, winning the hearts of many human beings they arrive into touch with, even supposing it's miles their first meeting.

This, in turn, consequences of their receiving a slew of accolades everywhere they bypass. As a quit result, whether or no longer or not at work, at social sports, at circle of relatives reunions, or in nearly any other putting, they get what they need, that is adoration and acclaim. However, now not like after they had been kids, this form of beauty isn't always coming from a superior determine figure however, as an alternative, from a hard and fast of inferior friends who've gathered spherical them. While this serves to enhance the narcissist's ego, additionally they may be inclined to understand it as perfectly low-cost. Because the narcissist considers themself to be the superior character in any state of affairs, it's far only sincere that everyone spherical them renowned this and feed their pressure for adoration.

What You Play inside the Narcissist's World

Having received a better facts of what reasons narcissistic man or woman sickness, it is time to consider the questions: What changed into their motivation for trying to dominate your lifestyles? What thing did you play? And why did they make it so difficult a great manner to head away? The rationalization is as clean as it's miles complex: narcissistic deliver.

Narcissists want a non-forestall supply of those who

they are able to abuse and employ to maintain their inflated sense of self esteem. They get a kick out of bullying and manipulating individuals due to the fact they consider that is what they will be exceptional at. Because they need ordinary affirmation and praise, narcissists are frequently round people. You were a supply of delight and admiration for them. They dealt with you in a way making sure that they had been given the popularity and approval they sought. So, inside the beginning, they maximum in all likelihood positioned their remarkable foot ahead, delivered all in their remarkable tales, and confirmed you the superb part of their individual to "hook" you and make you revel in obligated to reward them at every opportunity. Once that they'd acquired your take transport of as right with and you've got been surely entranced via their excellent individual, they gently fed you praise here and there that allows you to make you experience that you have been certainly as accurate as they have been. You have been taken care of. You felt like an extension of them, which in the long run fueled your personal underlying narcissistic dispositions.

However, you have got been liable to making mistakes now and again. In flip, you were subjected to insults and disapproval. In an instant, you were deemed unworthy, and your abuser maximum likely distanced themself from you. Their technique of maintaining manage over your life, understanding how crucial their approval modified into to you, turn out to be to do that. These exchanges of manipulate supplied an vital feeling of control in your abuser— some thing they sought frequently. Being capable of make choices gave them a revel in of empowerment and bolstered their feel of superiority. It stepped forward their enjoy of dominance in pushing you round and making you experience horrific because of the truth you didn't comply with their hints. Overall, they were inquisitive about retaining you round quality to fulfill their non-public necessities.

Even in the event that they expressed feelings of affection and affection for you, it's far viable that they have got been concerned handiest in gaining your take delivery of as authentic with and loyalty, and not in a few element else. Keep in mind that a narcissist is involved best with themselves. They are driven by means of the use of their preference for reputation, praise, and strength, which fuels the whole lot they do and say. Never neglect that you don't have anything to do with the narcissist's moves. Because of your moves, they've got treated you unfairly. The fact is, they may be toxic because of their non-public person. This is not your fault, and you have not any responsibility to correct the scenario. Consequently, refrain from apologizing to them or in search of to rationalize their occasions. Take care of your self first and essential. Value your self a protracted manner more extraordinarily than you price all and sundry else. If a person tells you that you're being egocentric through trying to attend to yourself, bear in thoughts that self-love is love and is virtually as crucial as every other shape of affection you may provide to everyone else. You, extra than everybody, are deserving of your hobby and remedy.

Chapter 7: What Happens After Leaving A Narcissistic Abuser

Perhaps the maximum hard component you have ever needed to do end up go away your narcissistic abuser. The relentless nagging, the in no manner-finishing shame, the regular pressure positioned on your decrease returned to offer them with some element that modified into already too hard to provide were all viable motives. The maximum critical thing to recognize is that you made the quality accurate selection, irrespective of what your motivation was. To recover from a dating with a narcissist, the only real solution is to move far from the scenario. Although you'll likely have heard and take a look at all of this from severa locations, you would in all likelihood in spite of the truth that find yourself teetering on the edge of feeling responsible. You want a go returned experience, similarly to an possibility to apologize. To pacify the narcissist, you need to tell them that they have been accurate and which you were incorrect. While the preference to return is probably outstanding, you have to recognize that the voice for your thoughts encouraging you to go back is a system that the narcissist set in location over the years you were together. This is how they were capable of carry out their motive of subjecting you to all of this abuse with the aid of the usage of way of creating you doubt your self confidence and making you revel in as if you owed them for every desire you made.

Being Aware of Your Emotions

It's likely which you're experiencing some of feelings in the in the meantime, this is making the technique difficult to navigate. You is probably questioning if you made the proper desire.

Following are some capability motives for the sensations and thoughts you is probably experiencing, that will help you placed subjects into perspective:

Guilt

Even even as were all in the domestic abuse and the narcissist located the duty for the entirety in your shoulders? You had been their scapegoat, and that they desired to look you are taking responsibility for all the terrible activities that happened in your existence collectively because it made them sense better approximately themselves. Unless you get popularity from your abuser, this relentless blaming will expand, for your mind, the idea that you are wrong about the whole lot you do. As a stop end result, in case you and your companion aren't on speakme terms proper now, you could locate your self berating yourself for the outcomes of your conduct. Please preserve in thoughts that everybody who crosses a narcissist might be inherently disliked, notwithstanding the truth that they've excellent reasons for doing so.

An loss of capability to understand their non-public faults reasons narcissists to get speedy enraged or even adversarial in the direction of every person who suggests that they have got finished something incorrect of their lives.

Unquestionably, having the strength to rise up for your self and say "sufficient" modified proper into a courageous preference, and moreover you need to be satisfied with your self for doing so. Keep your inner system from causing you to show spherical and question your choices. Nothing subjects besides that you move on and maintain your head above water.

Isolation

You might possibly have attempted speakme with buddies or own family humans approximately the modern changes on your reference to your abuser, but you could have been unsuccessful. They would possibly boom their brows in protest if they are additionally human beings of the narcissist's social circle, so keep a watch out for them. They might possibly ask, "Why could you go out of your manner to perform a little aspect like this?"

Before spending all your electricity attempting to justify why you felt it essential to do what you probably did, hold in thoughts that maximum folks who apprehend narcissists super on the floor receive as actual with they're immaculate. Take the subsequent example.

Earlier this year, Andy ended her courting with an vintage college mate whom she regarded as one in every of her closest buddies from lower decrease returned within the day. With her regular criticism about specific people, disparaging of other human beings's accomplishments, and attempts to exert manage over Andy's expert selections, Carol had end up toxic to be spherical. As a end result of the humiliation and everyday nagging she turn out to be experiencing, Andy ultimately decided that it turn out to be time to find out new pals, individuals who might assist her instead of tear her down. Consequently, she knowledgeable Carol that she might be taking a vacation from their regular regular and that she can be busy within the subsequent months as she have grow to be acclimated to her new role within the industrial organisation business organization. Unfortunately, Carol emerge as capable of decide out what Andy end up as masses as, and he or she or he proceeded to completely reduce off all communique collectively with her and their dating. Besides that, she made contact with each and each one in each of their not unusual buddies to tell them about what had passed off.

Everybody might be vulnerable to blame Andy for the dissolution of their friendship in this example. Andy, as an alternative, had lower lower again to her native land to spend the weekend collectively together with her parents. They knew Carol because of the truth she became really one among Andy's great friends, and that they believed she changed right into a outstanding individual. When her parents placed out that Andy and Carol had been now not on pleasant terms, they had been shocked.

However, despite Andy's nice efforts to relay the reality approximately Carol, what she come to be in reality like in the back of the smiles and the polite veneer, her parents could not receive a word she said. They clung to their preconceived notions about Carol, arguing that Andy had truly misinterpreted her buddy's motives. For Andy, the situation is probably identical from each standpoint, with all of the friends she shared with Carol adopting a similar mind-set, in particular due to the reality Carol had already supplied her component of the tale to them. Andy can be handled with each skepticism or grievance if she attempted to find someone to assist her in restoration from the separation. It might likely seem like a prolonged and lonely adventure to get over narcissistic abuse. Many of the human beings you expected to be there for you thru these hard instances won't be there the least bit, siding with the narcissist and telling you that you were maximum possibly answerable for all that has befell. Take coronary coronary heart, but, as the ones costs are not frequently proper.

In the equal way which you were conditioned to assume a selected way, it is possible that the narcissist have become able to have an impact at the manner your friends and circle of relatives people concept. On the floor, you may probable declare that the narcissist has succeeded in shielding their image from all factors of view, making sure that no one can see the fact, notwithstanding the truth that there's a person (which include your self) who can see that fact. There are severa forums and online organizations that you could want to sign up for to get the help you are attempting to find for. It might also additionally furthermore be beneficial to are trying to find the advice and help of a counsellor or therapist within the direction of your healing adventure. four .1 DISBELIEF

It's hard to understand how they will have done this form of detail. When you were however under the manipulate of the narcissist, you could have believed that the whole lot they finished modified into not anything short of surprising. But that become then. This is now. They had your outstanding pursuits at coronary heart, and the whole lot they advocated you to do have end up done so out of a strong choice to look you be triumphant. Nevertheless, after the haze has cleared, you is probably able to understand what they were definitely seeking to do. In this degree, the good intentions begin to resemble personal agendas, and the advice supposed to better your life starts offevolved to appear blatantly self-serving. The offspring of a narcissist are regularly folks that revel in the maximum disbelief. The truth that our dad and mom had been making demands to in shape their private goals in preference to offering tips to enhance their children's future comes as a marvel to the ones human beings who've been raised believing that our mother and father pleasant favored the quality for us.

Because their narcissistic trends will be predisposed to overcome their urge to be demanding and loving, narcissistic parents may appear unusual of their moves. They become manipulating their youngsters, giving them conditional affection, and pushing them to toe a strict line with a purpose to boom youngsters whom they could talk with as extensions in their very very very own personalities. As they get higher, you need to remember that the whole thing the narcissist did in the course of your dating have grow to be nearly truly completed for his or her personal benefit and which you have to take delivery of it. Although these gadgets may also have come as a wonder at the same time as you first identified them and as you continue to find out the reality, accepting the horrible reality of a narcissistic person will make it simpler to deal with the reality of their behavior.

Longing

In many instances, the outstanding trouble that saved you going was your desire to please and be praised thru the person who had abused you. The tiny quantities of "love" that they might fling at you gave you legitimacy and rate, loads as a canine craving for a bone would give you validation and nicely well worth. The instances whilst you

178

obtained even a semblance of love from your companion were greater than sufficient to maintain you going, no matter the toxic nature of your dating. So, the abuser managed to preserve you close by thru using providing you with conditional love and validation in little doses. This became an efficient approach to hold you searching for to cause them to satisfied whilst additionally retaining you associated with them. The unlucky fact is that now that the abuser isn't always spherical and you've got been left on this lonely scenario, you may haven't every body to expose to for the love you looking for. This is sometimes the toughest sensation to address: the yearning for some component to fill the void left via the usage of your abuser's departure. If the individual you had to leave changed into a narcissist, do not be worried; it is commonplace to look for someone else to take their characteristic.

You're best human, and a relationship it is ended continues to be a courting it's ended, regardless of the occasions. Nonetheless, you must maintain your composure in this situation. Realize that the love that your abuser turn out to be deliv- ering to you changed into now not in reality love and which you are surely appearing on the mechanism they installation to make you need a excellent form of love in the first place. It is likewise vital to understand that you are greater liable to clinging to every special narcissist than you have were given ever been in advance than. A new "remarkable individual" might probably make it heaps more hard to keep away from falling into the entice in case you meet them at a 2d at the same time as you're sensitive and emotional. Always be cautious of the people you meet and preserve an eye fixed fixed steady out for signs and symptoms of narcissism, which is probably diffused at instances. Instead of focusing on the advantages of loving someone else, maintain in thoughts the advantages of loving your- self. Being the number one character to recognize and recognize all of the exceptional factors of your non-public person will help you recognize that you do not need all people else's approval or affection.

Resolving the Situation with Your Abuser

As a stop cease result of your a fulfillment breakup with the narcissist, you is probably thinking whether or not or now not it's miles applicable to maintain any form of interaction with this man or woman. It might not be possible to completely near your doorways to an abuser, regardless of how lots you need to accomplish that. You will although have the potential to talk with immediate own family people, colleagues, and distinctive humans. What do you watched your possibilities are of being diplomatic for your interactions with them? As an area to start, no man or woman anticipates you searching for to "easy matters up" with a person who's narcissistic. However, if you recall that a civil dating is the nice healthy for the situations of your dating, it might be viable to gain achievement in those endeavors.

Second, with regards to being civil with a narcissist, it is viable to accomplish that. However, it is controversial whether or now not or not or no longer they'll be capable of adapting to or comprehending this. The offending party want to make an apology and apologize earlier than the connection can be restarted. Of course, the offending birthday party will in no way take delivery of duty for their movements, as a narcissist will in no way do the kind of trouble. If you do no longer make an apology, a narcissist may likely refuse to act politely in response in your actions. In your case, what does that entail? Simply located, a "civil" dating is probably definitely one-sided.

A narcissist, but, may additionally use any opportunity to embarrass you in case you try to initiate any sort of contact. In the case of a family get-collectively, as an instance, you may acquire out to speak about it, and the narcissist may also really dismiss you or overlook approximately your attempts to speak. If there are others present who can witness you being dealt with with hostility, this is something they're much more likely to do. Seeing as how the narcissist is in all likelihood to have an impeccable recognition among the ones round you, individuals who witness you being treated negatively will likely component with the narcissist, believing it's far your fault. It is commonly agreed that the only manner to deal with a toxic associate is to keep away from them completely. The narcissist can be handled as a non-entity, which can be an extended manner more beneficial to your highbrow and physical health. Ignoring them may be extraordinarily useful. Heal your self on an emotional level. This method now not high-quality prevents you from being drawn all over again into the narcissist's trap, but additionally ensures that the abuser cannot make the maximum you. How smooth do you decided it will probably be? In no way, form, or form! The urge to achieve out, to speak approximately matters, and to make an apology has been noted via severa sufferers of narcissistic abuse at every thing within the recuperation way, or even years after the relationship has ended.

This might be a difficult challenge, but it isn't insurmountable. These strategies will assist you on your recuperation way and will help you preserve a healthful distance from the person who harmed you. All conversation venues want to be closed. Delete your social media money owed. Unfriend and block humans on social media. It might possibly seem cruel, and in modern day virtual generation, it's miles absolutely the worst element you can do to someone on social media, but slicing off any channels of verbal exchange that you or they may use to attain out may be a super method to reduce the chance of the flame being rekindled. "But what if I want to speak with them inside the destiny?" Don't allow the possibility of some thing going wrong inspire you to keep those channels of verbal exchange.